RETHINKING
THE MUSEUM

RETHINKING THE MUSEUM

AND OTHER MEDITATIONS

STEPHEN E. WEIL

SMITHSONIAN INSTITUTION PRESS

WASHINGTON AND LONDON

Editor: Michelle Smith
Designer: Linda McKnight

Library of Congress Cataloging-in-Publication Data

Weil, Stephen E.
    Rethinking the museum and other meditations / Stephen E. Weil.
        p.   cm.
    Includes bibliographical references.
    ISBN 0-87474-948-4 (alk. paper).—
    ISBN 0-87474-953-0 (pbk.: alk. paper)
        1. Museums—Management.   2. Museum techniques—Evaluation.
    I. Title.
    AM7.W393   1990
    069'.5—dc20   89-21985

British Library Cataloguing-in-Publication Data is available

Manufactured in the United States of America

97 96 95 94 93 92 91 90   5 4 3 2 1

⊚ The paper used in this publication meets the minimum
requirements of the American National Standard for Perma-
nance of Paper for Printed Library Materials Z39.48–1984

For Wendy

CONTENTS

REPOSE AND OTHER BRIEF LEGAL NOTES

ACKNOWLEDGMENTS

While I have characterized the pieces in this book as "meditations," their origins have been in anything but solitary contemplation. The starting point for most was in a continuing and often vigorous discourse with a wide range of colleagues both within and without the domain of museums.

As a source and testing ground for ideas, three committees—one planning, and two advisory—with which I've had the good fortune to serve for a number of years have proven to be particularly important. Foremost in length of service is the Planning Committee for the American Law Institute–American Bar Association (ALI-ABA) annual Course of Study in the Legal Problems of Museum Administration. With a slowly shifting membership, that committee has been meeting since 1972. Through 1989, it had prepared and presented seventeen annual workshops of two-and-a-half days each at a variety of locations throughout the United States. The other members of the committee at this writing—all of them attorneys who have represented museums—are Lauryn Guttenplan Grant, Philip C. Jessup, Jr., Marie C. Malaro, Peter G. Powers, Marsha S. Shaines, Alan D. Ullberg, Nicholas D. Ward, Linden H. Wise, and Beverly M. Wolff. I'm grateful to them all.

Equally important has been the impact on my thinking of the Museum Management Institute (MMI) Advisory Committee, a body more fully described in the article about MMI's genesis and its early years that appears at pages 131–140. While the extract from the MMI Curriculum Statement entitled "The Well-Managed Museum" that appears at pages 69–72 was put into its final written form by Earl F. Cheit and myself, the thinking it embodies evolved over a period of years as a group product of this committee (most recently: Robert B. Andrews, Malcolm Arth, Earl F. Cheit, Signe Hanson, Charles F. Hummel, Pamela L. Myers, Jane G. Rice, Harold Skramstad, Jr., and myself). Also working with us on the development of the MMI Curriculum Statement were Philip Nowlen, the director of MMI; Harold Williams and Lani Lattin Duke of the J. Paul Getty Foundation; and Myrna Smoot and Ricki Lederman of the American Federation of Arts. The learning curve has been a long one. For several of us, the experience of working together on the launch and first flights of MMI dates back to June 1977.

A more recent involvement—but equally a stimulus, particularly to my thinking about cultural institutions other than museums—has been my membership on the Advisory Board of the Research Center for Arts and Culture at Columbia University, an interdisciplinary project that combines elements from Columbia's Business School, its graduate School of the Arts, and my own alma mater, the School of Law. Presided over by Joan Jeffri, director of Columbia's Graduate Program in Arts Administration, the committee's other members have most recently included Mary V. Ahearn, William Baumol, Paul DiMaggio, Ronald Feldman, Anthony Keller, Harold Klein, and Barbara Weisberger. The 1985 fragment "A Meditation on Work" at pages 167–169 was generated by one of the Research Center's earliest projects. Joan Jeffri was also responsible for soliciting the review of *The Arts and Public Policy in the United States* that appears at pages 141–146.

At the individual level, I am deeply indebted to a worldwide network of colleagues and friends. In Canada, Sheila Stevenson of the Nova Scotia Museum in Halifax gave the impetus to what eventually became "The Proper Business of Museums: Ideas or

Things?" In Australia, it was Caroline Turner of the Queensland Art Gallery who was first responsible for my preparing "In Pursuit of a Profession: The Status of Museum Work in America." In England, Peter Cannon-Brookes of *The International Journal of Museum Management and Curatorship* has been a constant encouragement.

United States colleagues and friends who have either helped to birth or groom some of the pieces in this book include Constance Lowenthal of the International Foundation for Art Research in New York; Elaine Heumann Gurian, once of the Children's Museum in Boston, but now my co-worker at the Smithsonian; and Gail Anderson of the Center for Museum Studies at John F. Kennedy University in San Francisco. Throughout, Milton Stern—dean of the University Extension at the University of California, Berkeley—has been a patient sounding board for some ideas about museums that later proved to be both good and bad. John Henry Merryman of the Stanford Law School has done much the same with respect to some legal concepts of concern to museums. To my companion Joan Wendy Luke, I can only say the most profound thank you for all of her tact, personal understanding, and critical insight.

At the Smithsonian Institution Press, the smooth passage of this book from concept to concrete form was effected by a wonderful assembly of talented individuals. With the sympathetic support of the Press's director Felix Lowe, managing editor Ruth Spiegel and acquisitions editor Amy Pastan took immediate charge of the project. Working directly with me on the text was my prescient and second-sighted editor Michelle Smith, who often understood how I meant to say things before I even knew what it was I wanted to say. For the book's design, I am deeply grateful to Linda McKnight.

Nothing in this volume would have been possible, however, except for a Smithsonian Institution tradition that permits and encourages its staff members to write, to teach and—as a necessary concomitant—also to reflect. It has been my enormous good fortune to have been in such a situation for the years necessary to produce this and its predecessor volume. The two directors of the Hirshhorn Museum and Sculpture Garden under whom I have worked since 1974—first Abram Lerner and then, following his retirement in 1984, James T. Demetrion—have been more than supportive of these efforts. As important has been the contribution of Carole Clore, my secretary and assistant for many years. Her patience with my constant rewriting (and sometimes wholesale recasting), her willingness to serve as a responsive and on occasion highly critical first reader, her extraordinary memory and her ingeniously resourceful abilities as a researcher are all reflected in the material that follows.

To all of them, and to the many other colleagues that space does not permit me to name, my heartfelt thanks. I can only hope that the product will prove worthy of their help. If not, the fault will have been mine. Their part was superb.

S.E.W.

PREFACE

While the pieces collected here were written over the relatively brief period of seven years, they vary enormously in style and even in their scholarly apparatus. Some tend toward the bare and laconic while others are generously footnoted. Some warmly address my museum colleagues as "we" while others maintain a cold and third-person impersonality. Some are humorous, a few are solemn. The genesis of this diversity lies in the diverse occasions for which they were first written as well as, in some instances at least, in the vagaries of their subsequent publication. I can only trust that their readers will find the resulting mix to a degree pungent and not too perplexing.

What should, though, I hope be clear is the consistent intention with which these writings began. It was to explore both for myself and for my audiences how the tangible and intangible resources that are available to museums—their collections and facilities, the scholarly and technical expertise of their staffs, and the indisputably high community prestige which they enjoy—might better be used. The use envisioned was that formulated by the International Council of Museums (ICOM) in its 1974 definition of museums—that such institutions be "in the service of society and of its development." Fundamental to my inquiry was the conviction that the museum itself is not some archetypical form that we who work in it are striving to bring into being but, rather, a constantly evolving social artifact that, for the moment, is ours to shape. In the words I have elsewhere quoted from Adele Silver's *The Art Museum as Educator,* "museums are inventions of men, not inevitable, eternal, ideal, nor divine. They exist for the things we put in them, and they change as each generation chooses how to see and use those things."

In revisiting the pieces that compose the first two sections of this book, three themes seemed to emerge as pervasive. The most fundamental of these was the need for specificity in considering the present condition or potential prospect of any particular institution or group of institutions. The universe of museums is enormous. At ICOM's 1989 triennial meeting in The Hague, it was suggested that there might be as many as forty thousand museums in operation worldwide. While none of us has ever visited more than a small fraction of that number, it seems virtually certain that the differences among those forty thousand museums—differences of scale, discipline, audience, history, ideology, format, financing, context, and purpose—must far exceed whatever elements they may have in common.

Nevertheless (and for the largely political reasons more fully elucidated in "The Proper Business of the Museum: Ideas or Things?" at pages 43–56), we have too often chosen to ignore the very rich ways in which museums differ and to focus instead on their thin margin of overlap. That we should do so is ironic. Among the most distinctive features of museums is that they deal with the specific and not the general, with what cannot simply be read or talked about but what must be actually seen or felt. Art museums, for example, hang neither the idea of a painting nor the average or median of all paintings nor even (except, perhaps, when swayed too far by the example of the natural history museum) the specimen type of a period, movement, or artist's lifetime output. What they hang are specific and tangible objects, important not principally in their commonality with other objects but for their own unique and irreducible qualities as works of art.

Museums ought be approached in a similar way. They ought

not be valued for the closeness with which they conform to the pattern of some ideal museum but, on the contrary, in each instance celebrated for what it is about them that is special and different. To consider them en masse is almost invariably to lose sight of what in them is most valuable. As William Blake long ago observed—see "Deaccessioning Modern and Contemporary Art: Some Notes on the American Experience" at page 119—"To Generalize is to be an Idiot. To Particularize is the Alone Distinction of Merit."

A second theme that runs through the first two sections of this book involves the issue of "professionalism." George Bernard Shaw once suggested that *all* professions were conspiracies against the laity. While this may well overstate the case (or equally well may not), I have found myself increasingly distressed by the incessant (and occasionally almost ritualistic) reiteration of the word "professional" in recent museum publications, conferences, and symposia. That the *concept* of professionalism (no less its quest) may have enormous value to the museum field seems beyond question. (For an effort to define that value more precisely, see "In Pursuit of a Profession: The Status of Museum Work in America" at pages 75–89.) It does not follow from that, however, that the public ought willy-nilly accept the claim that those of us who work in museums are therefore engaged in a "profession" and thereby entitled to some greater respect than ordinary people who merely hold jobs or follow occupations. That museum work might ultimately achieve such an elevated status is entirely possible. In my own view, however, it still has a great distance to go.

The third of these pervasive themes deals with the potential purposes of museums. During the seven-year span that these pieces cover, my own approach to thinking about museums has changed considerably. In *Beauty and the Beasts*—an earlier series of essays published by the Smithsonian Institution Press in 1983—my focus had been chiefly on the functions of museums: to collect, preserve, study, exhibit, and interpret collections. The inquiry there was centered on *what* museums did, not on *why* they did it. The latter, of course, is a far thornier matter. No internal political blood is likely to be spilled in making the decisions that collections ought be kept neat and orderly or that records should always be up to date. By contrast, deciding whether the program of a particular museum ought be supportive or questioning of the dominant culture—or even, assuming the same to be possible, that the museum ought observe a strict neutrality—is the very stuff of conflict. Yet it is precisely such difficult and potentially divisive questions that must be dealt with if museums are truly to play any significant role "in the service of society and of its development."

Throughout the museum field, there lately seems to have been a perceptible shift in focus away from the more technical aspects of day-to-day museum operations and toward the more fundamental questions of what a museum's purpose might be and what actual outcomes a museum might hope to achieve among its visitors and in its community. There are several possible explanations for this. Such a shift could, for example, relate to the maturation of the American Association of Museum's accreditation program—inaugurated in 1970, and now approaching its third decade—which increasingly examines the effectiveness of museum programs rather than merely ascertaining whether they are carried out at a threshold level of competence. Alternately, it might relate to the fact that the museums of the United States are far more technically adept today than in prior years and that previous questions as to their proficiency are no longer so pressing. Or it might relate to a pressure felt across the entire spectrum of nonprofit organizations to become accountable not merely for the resources entrusted to their care but also for the results achieved through their use of those resources.

Regardless of the reason, however, the museum field appears increasingly concentrated today on questions of ends rather than means. Having developed an enormous competence at collecting, preserving, and all the rest, toward what ends is that competence now to be used? While the specific answer may differ from museum to museum, the ICOM formulation nonetheless suggests that common to all such answers must be a purpose ultimately "in the service of society and of its development." Absent such a purpose, an institution—whatever else it may be—is beyond the boundary of what we define as a museum.

The final section of this book deals, albeit briefly, with a variety of legal topics that impinge on museums. Mindful, still, of Shaw's suggestion that the law, too, might be a profession that conspires against the laity, I have tried to avoid technical jargon and dared, even, to hope that the lay reader might find enchantment in some of the law's more esoteric manifestations. Like a good museum exhibition, these pieces are offered in the hope that they may entertain even while they instruct.

Such legal materials, however, have been included for another reason as well. In ways that I am not yet fully able to articulate, I have for some years had a growing sense that museums and the law are connected as part of some larger social process. Humankind is still at an early stage of learning how to manage itself. It has yet fully to understand how its members might best get on with one another or how they can best bring their needs into some kind of balance with the resources that they have available. There seems little question that the notion of heritage—what Klaus Schreiner has defined as "humankind's natural and social legacy"—has a vital part to play in this learning process. Without the accumulated heritage passed on to our own generation, we would have nothing upon which to build further. Without the means to pass that received heritage along to future generations, our own efforts to preserve and enhance it would ultimately prove to have been a waste.

Notwithstanding the enormously different ways in which they do so, museums and the law—and a whole host of other institutions besides—may be considered as agents for the preservation and transmission of heritage. As such, their work is critical. More than three centuries ago, Thomas Hobbes warned us in the most vivid language of what we might expect without a structure of civility in which to live our lives together: "No arts; no letters; no society; and which is worst of all, continual fear and danger of violent death; and the life of man, solitary, poor, nasty, brutish, and short."

It is here perhaps that the roles of museums and the law can finally be perceived as intertwined. As agents for the preservation and transmission of heritage, both can be counted as among those forces that stand against a life that might otherwise turn "solitary, poor, nasty, brutish, and short." Considered thus, understood in their roles as preservers and transmitters of heritage, museums and the law can each be seen as institutions of prime importance—worthy, at their best, of profound respect and, when they *are* at their best, a source of immense pride for those of us who are fortunate enough to work with and for them.

RETHINKING
THE MUSEUM

ENOUGH MUSEUMS?

The recent announcement that New York City would soon get a new museum of contemporary art prompted at least one observer to wonder: When will there finally be enough museums?

The question is not wholly idle. Since the end of World War II, museums have been one of the cultural scene's fastest-growing segments. According to a recent study commissioned by the federal government's Institute of Museum Services, more than half the museums in the United States were founded after 1950. During the thirty years ending in 1980, a period of some 1,566 weeks, nearly 2,500 new museums opened their doors. The rate was better than one each week. (For the United Kingdom, with a smaller population, the growth rate for the 1970s was equally impressive: A new museum opened every other week.) At such a rate, one might well wonder when the last bit of earth will have been appropriated to museum use and the last available visitor pressed into service as a trustee, docent, curator, or custodian.

In all likelihood, not for a while. For all the space they occupy in the media, museums have thus far made only the shallowest dent in reality. Nonetheless, the forces that have

ARTnews, 82(10). December 1983. This was originally written as a column for the magazine's "Perspective" series.

driven them to proliferate so dramatically show no sign of slackening. Foremost among these has been the quickening pace of invention. Since the beginning of this century, successive new technologies in transportation, computation, and communication have consistently stimulated the creation of new museums intended to preserve the specimen objects that embody their histories. Consider, for example, the Smithsonian's National Air and Space Museum in Washington.

With nearly ten million visitors annually, the Air and Space Museum is today the most heavily attended museum in the United States, if not the world. When the century began, prototypes existed for no more than a handful of the twenty-five thousand objects in its collection. Of equally recent origin are the contents of other new museums. On Boston's Museum Wharf a relocated computer museum has now settled in beside the Children's Museum; midtown Manhattan saw the establishment of the Museum of Broadcasting in 1975; and automobile museums abound—from the Auburn-Cord-Duesenberg Museum in Auburn, Indiana, to the Four Wheel Drive Foundation in Clintonville, Wisconsin. For those whose tastes run more toward self-propulsion, Lincoln, Nebraska, boasts a National Museum of Roller Skating.

Internal migration has also been a powerful impetus toward the proliferation of American museums. While the newly flourishing Sunbelt was drawing people away from the older cities of the East, the long-established eastern museums (decentralized in their governance and not easily susceptible to national planning) stayed behind. What moved the Brooklyn Dodgers out of Ebbets Field was not sufficient to move the Brooklyn Museum off Eastern Parkway. Sundered from their childhood museums, the new settlers in California, Texas, and Florida had no choice but to build new ones. This they have done with enthusiasm. In 1979, the *Official Museum Directory* listed 311 museums in California. For 1983, the figure was 367, an increase equal to better than one new museum every month.

As new museums multiply, the collections of old ones expand. In the typical natural history museum—the only kind of museum that can theoretically hope to "complete" its collection—only a fraction of the biota that might ultimately be collected has thus far been gathered. In the face of a rapidly degrading environment, to collect what remains outstanding has become an urgent task. Art and history museums—which together constitute nearly two-thirds of American museums—face a compound problem. As with natural history museums, there is a large body of already existing material that needs to be collected before it disappears. Beyond this, unprecedented quantities of art and new historic artifacts—many of which should eventually find repose in the sanctuary of a museum—continue to be generated with each passing day.

The United States Department of Labor now counts more than two hundred thousand Americans as artists. Hypothesize that each might annually create fifty works of art. A century of such activity will produce a billion paintings, sculptures, drawings, prints, and photographs. If art museums are to take a responsible sampling of what seems best from this outpouring, they must inevitably multiply and grow. As artists find new mediums with which to work—performance, holography, or computers—so much the greater will this burgeoning be.

Historic artifacts are no less like tribbles. Along with the detritus of great events—mugs that urge ratification of the Equal Rights Amendment, Rosalyn Carter's inaugural gown or a pro kit from World War II—history museums today also collect the material evidence of everyday life, whether Sandy Koufax's favorite glove or Archie Bunker's armchair. Add to this the mass of documentation made possible by the development of the camera, tape recorder, and video equipment, and it seems clear that history museums generally must either expand enormously or else spawn more specialized institutions that can share the burden of sorting through this glut to collect and preserve what most promises to be of value.

What seems to be common to all these situations—causing there to be new museums where before there were none, and making museums big when before they were little—is the constant of change: invention, movement and erosion, the search for the edges of art, and the irresistible unfolding of history. Is not this, though, just as it should be? Is not change, after all, what truly justifies every museum enterprise? In a timeless and static world, where everything was and would always be the way it had always been, museums would be superfluous. In a world from which nothing could ever disappear, there would be no need to be certain that some things were preserved.

To respond, then, to the original inquiry: When will there finally be enough museums? The answer has a millenary ring: When humankind has so mastered time that it no longer takes any toll, when the young are content to accept without change the world they will inherit from their elders, when artists ask nothing more than the opportunity to duplicate the works of their predecessors, when everybody believes that anything useful has already been invented and when the last restless migrant has settled on the last frontier, certain in the knowledge that no place better might lie beyond. In that best of all possible worlds, no more museums will be needed. Until then—and we may all join to hope that "then" may be a long way off—the unchecked, robust, and even boisterous proliferation and expansion of museums should not be a cause for concern. It is, rather, the signal of something healthy.

FIGHTING OFF SOME DRY ROT, WOODWORM, AND DAMP

F rom a hypothetically complete treatise on the operation of museums, I have imagined the following entry: "To assure the museum's future well-being, its physical premises should be examined periodically. By so doing, the staff can identify any areas where damage has occurred or deterioration may be in progress. It may also consider, in connection with such examination, whether any new building materials or equipment developed since the time of the facility's construction might be usefully incorporated into its structure." In support of such an imagined entry, AASLH's [American Association for State and Local History] *Bibliography on Historical Organization Practices* offers us such very concrete references as "Better Safe than Sorry," "Termite Control in History Landmarks," and "How to Combat Dry Rot, Woodworm, and Damp."

I

Our physical premises, however, are not the only ones that need to be examined periodically. From time to time, we must also

The original text from which this essay has been adapted was prepared for delivery at the 1985 annual meeting of the Southeastern Museums Conference, Charlotte, North Carolina, October 16, 1985. Reprinted, with permission, from *Museum News*, June 1986. Copyright © 1986, American Association of Museums. All rights reserved.

examine our intellectual premises. By these I mean that core of basic propositions concerning museums which, in their aggregate, shape not only our individual institutions but the very field itself. As you embark today on an extended consideration of the future of museums—not only for the balance of this century but for much of the next one as well—an examination of these premises could not be more timely. With the passage of the years, these premises too may become afflicted with "dry rot, woodworm, and damp." Like our physical premises, some of these premises as well may require periodic refinement, renovation or even, in the most extreme cases, replacement.

What I propose is to examine in some detail two premises which—sometimes articulated, but often not—have played important roles in the way we have thought about museums during the past ten to fifteen years. These are: that all museums are created equal, and that a strengthened professionalism should be the dominant principle around which to organize the operation of our museums.

For the reasons I will propose, it seems to me that each of these premises—no matter how sound or useful it might once have been—today stands in need of refinement, possibly of renovation, and conceivably of replacement.

II

"All museums are created equal." It is on that basis—and a fine, ringing, democratic basis it is—that we have, in recent years, operated our professional associations ("one museum, one vote"), framed our appeals to the Congress, and successfully energized our constituencies. For political purposes—and of necessity there are and will continue to be times when political considerations may be paramount—this notion that our institutions have a certain basic equality has proven attractive. It has also served to remind us that small museums as well as large can inspire wonder, elicit delight, meet the most demanding of technical standards and, in every way, achieve excellence.

Problems arise, though, when we attempt to employ this premise in other contexts. The difficulty is in that, as a proposition, it simply is not wholly true. It does not wholly conform to the facts. Museums differ, they differ enormously, and some of these differences—particularly in scale, in discipline, and in their relationships to their communities—are not merely differences of degree. They are differences of kind. The proposition that all museums are created equal blurs these differences in dangerous ways. To use individual museums as a unit of measure can lead us to false conclusions and ultimately distort not only the way *we* perceive ourselves but also the ways in which we are perceived by the public at large.

To see this vividly demonstrated, we need look no further than to the way in which a number of observers regard the accreditation program that the American Association of Museums established in 1970. Accreditation is available today to any otherwise qualified museum with an operating budget of $25,000 or more. According to the Institute of Museum Service's 1979 universe study—still the most recent source of figures we possess—in that year there were nearly 2,200 such museums in the United States. Presumably, there are more today. And yet, as of July 31, 1985, fifteen years after the program's inception, only 605 museums had qualified for accreditation—less than one-third of all those that were eligible. Further dashing the original hope that accreditation might ultimately become an all but universal standard for American museums is the startling decline in the number of museums now entering the program. Whereas 157 museums received accreditation in 1972, the number of newly accredited museums had sunk to 15 by 1981. It was back up to 31 in 1983, then last year again sank to 24.

Viewed through the eyes of equality, these are discouraging numbers. Using individual museums as a measure, and weighing them all alike, what we see is an accreditation program that was initially welcomed with great enthusiasm but since then has stalled. Certainly, viewed this way, it today seems a long way from fulfilling the high hopes that attended its birth.

On the other hand, if we look at accreditation through the eyes of reality, then a wholly different picture emerges. The 1979

IMS survey identified 164 museums which then had operating budgets of $1,000,000 or more. The number of museums with such budgets that are now accredited or in process stands at 156. Disregarding that some additional museums may have been added to the base since 1979, we find an accreditation rate among larger museums of just over 95 percent. Allowing for some additions to the base, the rate should still be above 90 percent. The AAM currently estimates that there are not more than ten museums throughout this country with million dollar or more budgets that remain unaccredited.

Even when we drop our focus down to museums with operating budgets between $500,000 and $1,000,000, we still find that the majority are accredited. Using estimates prepared by the AAM, of what might be up to 200 museums in this category, 107 are currently accredited. Employing real numbers—not counting museums one-by-one but weighting them for size—we find that the overwhelming proportion of museological activity in the United States is today carried out in accredited museums. In terms of major and medium-sized institutions—whether defined by budget, collections, or attendance—accreditation has been an enormous success. Using these same real numbers, though, we also have to ask whether accreditation has really proven an appropriate means to set standards for smaller organizations. Among nearly 600 museums in the IMS survey with annual budgets between $25,000 and $50,000, fewer than 3 percent are accredited. Might not some other approach for these—MAP and its extensions, for example—be more suitable? We cannot even begin to ask such a question, though, until we start to distinguish apples from oranges and stop treating them all the same.

Consider "Collections Management, Maintenance and Conservation," the recently completed study on the state of American museum collections which the AAM undertook for the IMS. Participating in this study were 364 museums with operating budgets ranging from $53,000,000 to $35,000. Think of that for a moment: $53,000,000 to $35,000. The ratio of the largest annual budget to the smallest was 1,514 to 1. This is no longer apples and oranges. This is more like diamonds and dinosaurs. And yet, in the published summary of the report, we still find that the individual museum—unmediated by any consideration of scale—is being used as a measure.

Thus, for example, we learn from the summary that only 26.4 percent of the museums sampled had a full-time conservator on staff. Which are the 73.6 percent that didn't? Were these larger museums that could afford one but elected not to? If so, then the public might be amply justified in believing that American museums are being negligent in the care of the collections with which they have been entrusted. Or were these predominantly smaller museums that either had no funds for a full-time conservator, could get by with a part-time one, or found it more economical to use outside consultants? If the latter was the case, then maybe what these figures would indicate is that—far from being negligent—American museums are frugal and well managed. As it is, though, the figure tells us neither of these. It tells us nothing.

Again, the summary reports that the 364 museums in the sample group held a total of 133,572,140 objects in their collections. It also reports that 30 percent of the sample museums had never surveyed any part of their collections for conservation purposes. Does this mean that 30 percent of these objects—40,000,000 or more—are held in museums that have not even bothered to examine their collections to ascertain their condition? If so, that might certainly be damaging to the public regard in which museums are held. Or are those museums that have wholly failed to survey their collections chiefly smaller ones with relatively minor holdings? Numbers generated on an "all museums are equal" basis at best tell us nothing. At worst, they obscure things we should know.

Nowhere, though, can this failure to discriminate among museums of different scale produce more dubious results than when the premise "all museums are equal" becomes a basis for public funding. And yet, given the pitifully small amount it has had available to provide general operating support, the IMS has had to do something nearly comparable to this since it was first established in 1976. In 1984, for example, limiting itself to a maximum grant of $50,000 or 10 percent of operating budget, whichever sum is smaller, the IMS was unable to make any distinctions whatsoever among the 330 or more American museums with budgets that exceeded $500,000. It could not even make significant distinctions between those and museums with lesser budgets. A grant of $48,000 to Reynolda House may be wholly explicable, but how can one explain a grant to the North Carolina Museum of Art of $50,000—only $2,000 more? Likewise, are the North American Wildfowl Museum in Salisbury, Maryland, and the Louisiana State Museum really such comparable organizations that the former should have gotten $49,703 and the latter $50,000, just $297 more?

In 1985, IMS raised its grant ceiling to $75,000. While this reduced the number of its grants from 530 to 449, it did mean that rationally proportional amounts could be awarded to museums with annual operating budgets of up to $750,000. Museums with larger budgets again had to be treated alike. To an outside observer, it might be entirely inexplicable why, for example, the Bass Museum of Art in Miami Beach was given the same grant of $75,000 as were such far larger institutions providing a correspondingly greater public service as Colonial Williamsburg, the Field Museum of Natural History, the San Diego Zoo, and the Metropolitan Museum of Art.

The fault, again, is not with IMS but with its slender share of the federal budget. Making the case for *more* funds might be easier if museums could project some clearer picture of the field, of who we are—not that all museums are equal and should be treated equally, but that museums come in a variety of types and sizes, collect to different degrees and in different ways, provide different services and have different needs.

What might well be worth considering is the development of a taxonomy of museums—a system of classification under which museums could be assigned to categories indicative of their scale and type. This has now been done in the field of post-secondary education. The Carnegie Commission on Higher Education published the first such classification in 1973. A revised version was published in 1976 by its successor, the Carnegie Council on Policy Studies in Higher Education. Each of 3,074 accredited institutions was assigned to one of nineteen categories. These ranged from Research Universities in categories I and II at the very top down through Liberal Arts Colleges toward the middle and then further down to two-year colleges and institutions for nontraditional study.

In making these assignments, quality was not the measure. Because of their relatively small size and because they lack graduate schools, some colleges generally considered among the finest in the country—Amherst and Bennington, for example—were placed in the seventh category, Liberal Arts Colleges I. Within any of the larger groups, the assignment of an institution to category I or II was not determined by any judgment as to the excellence of the education it offered but solely by objective, functional criteria. Thus, to qualify for the first category of Doctorate-Granting University, an institution would, among other things, have to award at least forty Ph.D. degrees in at least five different fields in the base year. Failing that, it could still qualify for the second category if it had awarded at least twenty such degrees without regard to field or ten or more degrees in at least three different fields. Some of the other criteria used for various categories included student enrollment, success in obtaining federal grant support for academic science and—perhaps most intriguing—the average SAT scores of an institution's incoming freshman class.

To illustrate how this worked for the eight categories covering universities and colleges, here are some random examples from the Southeast Region: Of fifty-one institutions nationally that were classified in the very top category, Research Universities I, three were in North Carolina: the University of North Carolina at Chapel Hill, North Carolina State University at

Raleigh and Duke University. Research Universities II included the University of Virginia's Main Campus and Vanderbilt University. Typical of those categorized as Doctorate-Granting Universities I were Clemson, the University of Southern Mississippi, and the University of Alabama. Doctorate-Granting Universities II included the University of South Florida and the College of William and Mary. Wake Forest, Furman, Marshall University, and Rollins College were classified as Comprehensive Colleges and Universities I while Washington-Lee University and Mary Washington College were ranked in category II. Finally, among four-year schools, Centenary College, Birmingham Southern, and Sweet Briar were ranked as Liberal Arts Colleges I, and the College of Charleston and High Point College typified those classed as Liberal Arts Colleges II. To repeat: these classifications were not judgments as to quality. (Clearly, a small institution may provide as good an education as a large one.) Their purpose was to further research and analysis in the field of higher education by a candid recognition that all institutions are not the same. They were established to permit like to be compared with like. They reduce the need to refer to diamonds and dinosaurs, or even to juggle apples and oranges.

What objective criteria might we employ to establish a taxonomy of museums? How might we begin to measure the degree of "museological activity" occurring in—or, more importantly, perhaps, the quantum of "museological service" being delivered by—a particular institution. Without suggesting what weight these various factors might be given—and recognizing at the outset that certain factors would have to be weighted differently for different disciplines—a thousand beetles is not a thousand lithographs is not a thousand antique automobiles—there are nonetheless some criteria on which everybody might be able to agree.

A museum's budget, for example, should generally be a good indicator of its level of activity. On the other hand, activity may not necessarily equate with result and budget size cannot be used alone. A museum's annual attendance, for instance, might tell something about the public service it delivers. But here, of course, we must be prepared to adjust for various levels of admission charges or for museums that charge no admission at all. Staff size might be a relevant indicator of *both* a museum's level of activity and the quantum of service it delivers. Likewise, the square footage available for different sorts of activities—exhibitions, storage, and conservation, for example—might give us some measurable insight by which to categorize an institution. So too could the size, types, and variety of its collections.

Other useful indicators might include the following: Salary—How does the museum's salary scale (adjusted, if need be, to eliminate regional differences) compare with those of other institutions of similar discipline and scale? Is it able to attract the best people in the field or must it settle for less? Publications—How many publications does the museum originate a year? How do the total pages it publishes annually compare with those published by other institutions of similar discipline and scale? Grants received—How are the museum's activities judged by the various federal, state, and private grant-making bodies to which it applies for funds? Staff education—How many advanced degrees are held, for example, by the one-third most highly paid employees, and how does this compare with other institutions of similar discipline and scale? One factor which might even be taken into account—and it's one that I've never seen in any major museum study—is the average length of visitation. I submit that a museum in which visitors generally tend to linger for two to three hours ought objectively be considered as rendering a greater quantum of museological service than one of comparable size in which visitors generally turn to leave after the first fifteen minutes.

These—and many more—are all objective tests. Daunting as the underlying calculations might once have been, they should today be easily within the range of a computer. They would take us as far, but no further than the colleges and universities have

thus far gone nor any further than such a cultural service organization as the American Symphony Orchestra League. It classifies
its members on the single criterion of annual budget and then
uses that classification as the basis for annual statistical studies
that are distributed back to its membership. With LORT—the
League of Regional Nonprofit Theaters—we find classification is
used differently. For purposes of its union agreement with Ac-
tor's Equity, LORT divides its membership into classes on the
basis of their average weekly box-office receipts.

Genuine courage, however, might be to take a step beyond
these mechanical tests—to factor in at least one criterion that
would arguably be subjective in its measurement: the significance of an institution's collection! All museums are not equal,
and neither are all collections equally significant.

How extraordinarily evolved the museum field might become if we could trust one another's good faith sufficiently to
permit such judgments to be made and to be made publicly. To
say that the Able Museum had a substantially more significant
collection than the Baker Museum would not—unless all other
things were equal—be to say that the Able was a better museum.
It might, though, suggest that the Able's ability to care for its
collection was a more appropriate matter for public concern (or
even public funding) than the Baker's ability. It could also suggest
that the Baker's best long-term strategies might revolve around a
program of loan exhibitions and the pursuit of acquisitions and
that those were the areas in which it could best make use of public
support. Until we get past our premise that all museums are
created equal and its inescapable corollary—that all collections
are equally significant—we truly face the possibility that, at some
outer and bizarre extreme, we may one day find a superbly
trained and managed staff working at the public's expense to give
the finest care imaginable to a large collection of no significance
whatsoever.

Even if we are not yet prepared to take this final step and
make the significance of collections a factor in classifying mu-

seums, the development of an objectively based museum taxonomy would still give us a far better understanding of our own
field. It could also be of enormous benefit to those who make the
public policies that affect museums as well as those foundations,
corporations, and government agencies that assist in their funding. If our academic colleagues can accept a system that assigns a
High Point College to a different category than a UNC at Chapel
Hill—not better, not worse, but different—then we ought be able
to accept something comparable that acknowledges that all museums may achieve excellence while permitting appropriate distinctions to be made on the basis of some very real differences.

III

As pervasive as the notion that all museums are created equal is
the conviction—among those who work in museums—that a
strengthened professionalism should be the cardinal principle
around which to organize the operation of museums.

Dr. Johnson once defined "patriotism" as the last refuge of a
scoundrel. Improving on this, that grand nineteenth-century
master of the art of political patronage, New York's Senator
Roscoe Conkling, suggested that Dr. Johnson had overlooked
what Conkling called the enormous possibilites of the word
"reform." I will reveal a bias of my own by further suggesting that
there are times when incessant appeals to the word "professionalism" strike me as the last refuge—not of scoundrels, certainly—
but of those who would prefer to be judged by friends and peers
in the museum world rather than by those under whose duly
constituted authority they are employed. Of that, more later.

For now, consider the story of the late (and, I think, la-
mented) China Trade Museum in Milton, Massachusetts, a community some nine miles south of downtown Boston. Founded in
1964 by H. A. Crosby Forbes, the museum occupied a Greek
Revival mission that had been built by Forbes's great-grandfather
Captain Robert Bennet Forbes in 1833. During the twenty years
after its founding, the museum's collection had grown to roughly
twelve thousand objects relating to—as one Boston reporter

described it—"Chinese commerce with the West during the golden age of the Yankee clipper ship." What had not grown was storage and display space adequate for the care of the collection. Instead the museum's cumulative operating deficit had grown. A $400,000 endowment had shrunk to $200,000, and a projected 1984 deficit threatened to shrink it still further. That the museum's financial position had so deteriorated does not seem to have been made known to the community at large.

In May 1984, the local newspapers disclosed that a committee of the museum's board of trustees had been quietly negotiating with the Peabody Museum of Salem—founded in 1799 and the oldest continuously operating museum in the United States—to see if the museum in Milton might not be merged into the museum in Salem, a seaport somewhat further to the north of Boston than Milton was to the south of it. As the terms of this proposed merger took shape, they seemed—as, indeed, they proved to be—irresistible. If the bulk of the China Trade Museum's collections were transferred to the Peabody, then, the latter would build a new 25,000 square-foot China Trade Wing to open in May 1987, with two anonymous donors contributing a total of $3,000,000 toward the construction and endowment of this new wing. The relevant collections of the Peabody Museum would be combined with those of the China Trade Museum to form an expanded department of Asian export art. And Crosby Forbes—the man who had founded the China Trade Museum some twenty years earlier—would become the head of this new department. Concurrently, the China Trade Museum would transfer its archival collection of roughly one hundred thousand eighteenth- and nineteenth-century documents to the Massachusetts Historical Society. Since the old Forbes mansion was itself immovable from Milton and couldn't be thrown into the deal, it would remain and—left with a small collection of decorative objects and family memorabilia—be turned over to another organization and operated as a historic house.

There were heated reactions back in Milton as this news emerged. The local selectmen held hearings to determine what might be done to keep the China Trade Museum in town. Within the museum's active group of volunteers, there was particular distress that "their" museum might so suddenly be whisked out from under them. A citizen's group calling itself the Friends of the China Trade Museum was formed, and one of its cochairmen, a local attorney, was authorized to explore what legal steps could be taken to block the merger. At the request of the Friends, the Massachusetts Attorney General's Office began its own investigation.

All this came to naught. No legal action was ever brought, the Attorney General's Office announced that it would not oppose the merger, and on September 24, 1984, the board of the China Trade Museum voted its final approval of the merger, 21 to 3. A week later, less than five months after news of the proposed merger had first begun to circulate, the museum closed its doors and left town.

What factors did the Attorney General's Office take into consideration when examining the proposed merger? Perhaps it reasoned that the move was wholly within Massachusetts: while there was a constituency in Milton that might consider itself deprived, there was an offsetting constituency in Salem that might consider itself benefited. And if the Attorney General's Office had consulted curators in the field, what other criterion might have been urged as paramount? Surely the professional consideration—the well-being of the collection. There was every reason to believe that the Peabody would care for the collection as well-or-better-than the China Trade Museum had cared for it back in Milton.

It is at precisely this point, however, that I find myself questioning whether this professional consideration ought not have been tempered by a different one, a consideration that rarely appears in recent discourse about museums. That is the consideration of community. How important is it that a museum may be a social nexus, that it may play a role as the place in which—and an activity through which—a community may give itself a particular identity and strength? How important is it that a museum is fundamentally a community organization? As one saddened lo-cal resident described the China Trade Museum: "It could offer something to Milton that was not parochial—it was certainly of national and international significance—and in that sense, it gave something to the community that nothing else does."

The community! In museum training programs, in the growing body of museum literature, even in the procedures for accreditation, how often do we focus on the need and the means to make museums more responsive to their communities? In our interactions with one another, we tend to be technicians. In formulating our programs, we are more apt to be cosmopolitan. And all too often, when we do finally look to the local public, it is only as the target of development efforts—to raise funds and promote membership.

In the Canadian Museums Association's widely used hand-book *Basic Museum Management,* the community is likened to a guest whom we invite to a banquet that we have prepared. The banquet is our program. We choose the dishes. Harder to find in the museum literature is advocacy of the notion that what we should present to our communities is not a banquet but a menu, a menu imaginatively composed of dishes for which we have the ingredients on hand and that meet our standards of taste but from among which the public can make choices. Sometimes, in the literature, it's scarcely possible to find any real consideration of the community.

Looking, for example, through the otherwise solid recom-mendations of *Museums for a New Century* shows that the word "community" is most often used in the context of "museum community" rather than with reference to those very real flesh and blood, brick and mortar communities in which we reside and from which of necessity museums must draw their sustenance. From these reiterated references to the "museum community," a skeptic might envision the museums of the United States—or, with a boost from ICOM, those of the whole world—ultimately fusing together into one great supermega museum and, escaped at last from the daily annoyance of donors, trustees, visitors, and local politicians, floating serenely up to some frictionless museological heaven where its cosmopolite staff would ever-after be free to collect, preserve, exhibit, study, and interpret in a clean, well-lighted place that was all its very own.

To a degree far greater than schools, libraries, or hospitals, museums tend to be—the phrase is Barry Gaither's—self-initiated. Other kinds of nonprofit organizations are often established to meet a perceived and definable community need. Not so museums. For the most part, a museum comes into being either to preserve an existing collection, to satisfy the philanthropic yearnings (or desire for immortality) of a founding donor, or in response to the interest of some energetic core of history, art, nature, or science enthusiasts. Yet no matter how it is founded, with rare exceptions the only way a museum can long continue is through the support it draws from its community. Not the museum community, but its own community. We who work in museums may all be a periodic comfort to one another—but we are not one another's life blood.

Perhaps at some level, this notion is distressing. And there may be a direct link between that distress and the degree to which we increasingly insist on the professional status of museum work. As I suggested earlier, one of the attractive features of such a claim is the thought that it might permit us to have our work judged by one another and not by outsiders. This seems, on its face, only fair. Why should the judgment of knowledgeable insiders not be preferable to the judgment of community members who may lack our special educations, subject-matter skills, and technical expertise? Alas, however, it is not each other's consent we need to continue in museum work, but the community's.

At no time does the museum world reveal its ambivalence about the local community more strongly than when faced with the necessity of marketing to that community. There is deep resistance, by no means a wholly unreasonable one, to the basic tenet of marketing—that it is more productive to shape a product to the needs of the market than to force a predetermined product on a market that may or may not feel any need for it.

The problem, of course, is that museums—almost uniquely among institutions—have at least one predetermined product: their existing collections. Marketing, though, may still be relevant—it remains a way to explore how this fixed set of ingredients might be used as the basis for a menu from which the public could make choices instead of having these collections set before it as a take-it-or-leave-it banquet. But, yes: A museum with a collection wholly of seashells in a community fascinated by nothing but sharks' teeth has a real problem that the basic propositions of marketing may do little to solve.

However, this resistance within museums to the concept of marketing goes beyond whatever hesitation might reasonably be based on the special situation of museums as institutions with existing collections. Mingled with it also seems to be a sort of fear, a fear that giving the community (the museum's major market) a more participative role in shaping programs might dilute our standards, or cheapen what we do, or leave us open to charges of pandering to the tasteless, the misguided, or the misinformed. Some of us become fearful, too, when we are urged—see, for example, the article by Michael Ames of the University of British Columbia's Museum of Anthropology in issue 145 of *Museum*—to democratize the operation of museums by giving users greater and more direct access both to the collections and to the information about these collections. To quiet such fears, it is tempting to raise the claim of professional status as a defense.

For many, this does double duty. The term "professional" distinguishes those who work in museums as staff from those who serve on the boards of trustees. Against what may seem to us their affluence or social position, we may counterpoise our own claim to the prestige of professional status. And framing certain issues as "professional" ones may seem to reserve the ultimate decision making to ourselves rather than to those ultimately responsible for museum management. The prestige may be real enough, but the responsibilities of the board remain the responsibilities of the board no matter how we frame such issues or what we call ourselves.

By no means, certainly, is this focus on professionalism recent. It was deeply intertwined in the process that led first to the publication of the *Belmont Report* in 1968 and then, in accordance with the *Report*'s recommendations, to the establishment of the AAM's accreditation program in 1970. Instructive here is the definition of a "museum" that was adopted for use in that program: "an organized and permanent nonprofit institution, essentially educational or aesthetic in purpose, with professional staff, which owns and utilizes tangible objects, cares for them and exhibits them to the public on some regular schedule."

While this definition makes a slight bow toward what it identifies as the museum's purpose—to be essentially educational or aesthetic—the main stress is functional. It emphasizes what museums do: they own objects, care for them, and exhibit them. It also specifies that this is to be done by a "professional staff."

By contrast, consider the definition of a "museum" that ICOM adopted at its 1974 meeting in Copenhagen: "A museum is a non-profitmaking, permanent institution in the service of society and of its development, and open to the public, which acquires, conserves, researches, communicates, and exhibits, for purposes of study, education and enjoyment, material evidence of man and his environment."

The stress here is different. The emphasis is on service and the museum's purposes. Functions are listed, but they are subordinate. The word "professional" does not occur at all.

In the end, of course, the functioning and purposes of museums are inseparable. To function without purpose would be meaningless, nor can any purpose ever be served except through the medium of a functional activity. Nonetheless, as these divergent definitions seem to suggest, the American museum community appears to have linked the notion of professionalism more closely to function than to purpose. In the case of the China

Trade Museum, the "professional" solution was the one that concentrated on the care of the collection, not the one that looked to the welfare of the community that the museum was intended to serve.

What really is required, of course, is a double concentration, and a balanced one. To raise these issues of purpose, service, and need is not to suggest that our aspiration to professionalism be abandoned, that our technical skills be allowed to fade, or that our standards be lowered. What it does suggest is that we must be bipolar in our thinking—that we must envision a higher professionalism, one in which museum staff members become as expert and skillful in responding to community needs and desires as they are today in collecting, preserving, studying, exhibiting, and interpreting collections.

Museums may be self-initiated, but—with rare exceptions—are not and cannot be self-perpetuating. We continue to function only with the consent of our communities. As Boston museum consultant Larry Morrison put it, "A museum cannot serve exclusively or even chiefly as a vehicle for the personal or professional fulfillment of its staff unless, of course, it wishes to ignore the requirements of public consent."

In *Museums: In Search of a Usable Future* (The MIT Press, 1970), Alma Wittlin put it more gently but no less firmly: "Museums are not ends in themselves; they are means in the service of man and his cultural evolution."

The premise that professionalism ought be the dominant principle in the operation of museums is, at best, too narrow. Professionalism is mostly about the people who work in museums. Service is about other people. It is for their collections and for other people, not just the people who work in them, that museums exist. The ideal balance of professionalism and community service may be different in museums of different scales and types. It may even be that these differences can account in part for the dramatic difference in the accreditation rates between the largest and smallest American museums: a rate of more than 90 percent for the former but no more than 3 percent for the latter. Those who work in small museums may have long since recognized (or perhaps have never forgotten) what some people who work in larger museums are only beginning to understand—that maintenance of professional standards, critical as that may be, cannot be substituted for a sense of community service if a museum is long to survive.

Whether these differences are real, whether there is or ought to be a different balance of these elements in different museums, cannot be fully explored until we get past the first of our two premises—that all museums are created equal—and begin to make some real distinctions about who we are and what we do.

A MEDITATION ON SMALL
AND LARGE MUSEUMS

I

When Joseph H. Hirshhorn died in 1981, he left the Hirshhorn Museum some six thousand works of art. These were in addition to another six thousand objects that he had contributed when the museum was founded in 1966. In short order, this second group of six thousand paintings, sculptures, and works on paper became a sort of litmus test, a handy device to distinguish those who were knowledgeable about museums from those who were not. Periodically, one of the latter would approach somebody on staff and remark, in the best of faith, "I understand that you just inherited another six thousand art works. How wonderful that must be!!" A museum colleague, by contrast, was more apt to ask "Did Joe Hirshhorn *really* leave you another six thousand things?" When the answer was affirmative, the customary response was a self-slap to the inquirer's cheek followed by a sympathetic and doleful "Oy!" We were not about to get six thousand masterpieces. In the field of contemporary art, there may not even *be* six thousand masterpieces.

The point, of course, is that those of us who work in mu-

This text was originally delivered as a talk to the Western Museums Conference meeting in Portland, Oregon, in September 1987. It was subsequently printed in the *Museum Studies Journal*, Vol. 3, No. 2 (San Francisco: John F. Kennedy University Center for Museum Studies, 1988).

seums understand that a large collection can be a mixed blessing. On the positive side, it provides an important argument for maintaining institutional continuity, it may frequently be a source of prestige, and—perhaps most important—in the current theology of American museums, to own and to care for a collection is to fulfill what has come to be regarded as our fundamental purpose. In the official view, our very museumhood has—for the most part—been all but equated with the acquisition and care of a collection.

On the other hand, as all of us know, a large collection will often include much that may be of little or no long-term interest. Not every object ever evolved or created can justifiably be preserved in however close to perpetuity we can manage. Beyond that, collections are demanding. They cost time and money to care for, they require space for storage, they need documentation and study, and, above all, they demand to be seen. Collections, moreover, tend to be static. The more heavily a static collection may weigh in the life of an institution, then the greater the danger that the institution itself may become static as well.

Nonetheless, the hypothesis that the acquisition and care of collections ought to be the central concern of every museum now dominates our rhetoric. In the American Association of Museums' (AAM) 1984 publication *Museums for a New Century,* for example, we read that ". . . collections are the essence of the contribution museums make to society." Elsewhere we read that the basic importance of museums lies in their role as the "stewards of a common wealth."[1]

In part, of course—and especially in the case of the AAM— this has been a strategy that has given museums a "niche," to use a favorite term of the marketeers. Consider the alternatives. If museums were to be presented fundamentally as a place for learning, then in the competition for public funds, they would find themselves pitted against a broad array of other and often stronger educational institutions. Likewise, if museums were to be presented essentially as centers for scholarship, the competing claims of universities and research centers might be difficult to overcome. And if museums were to be presented as potentially vital agents for social change, public funding might be frightened away entirely. Thus, in the competition for public funds, it has made a kind of strategic sense to stress what it is that is most distinctive about museums—that they acquire and care for collections.

The difficulty is that somewhere along the line too many of us—and here I must include myself—have too frequently misapprehended what has been a strategy to be the truth. We have too often taken what is a necessary condition to the work of museums—the existence of carefully acquired, well-documented and well-cared-for collections—and treated that necessary condition as though it were a sufficient condition. In developing justifications for the public support of museums, we have too often forgotten that their ultimate importance must lie not in their ability to acquire and care for objects—important as that may be—but in their ability to take such objects and put them to some worthwhile use. In our failure to recognize this, we run the danger of trivializing both our institutions and ourselves.

It is true, certainly, that many of our largest museums were originally established to be educational institutions rather than the enormous repositories they have since become. It is also true that the official museum theology is properly deferential to the educational roles that museums can and do play. Indeed, four of the sixteen recommendations in *Museums for a New Century* address that point directly. Nonetheless, education has become, in all too many of our largest institutions, a limping afterthought about how a collection might be employed instead of the motivating forethought that would determine just what should be collected in the first place. Is it any surprise then that, among art museums at least, curatorship has clearly outstripped any other museum occupation as the background from which museum directors have most frequently been selected?[2] Likewise, is it any wonder that, in their 1986 study *The Uncertain Profession*, Elliot Eisner and Stephen Dobbs report that, again in art museums, educators perceived themselves "as having little or no power to shape . . . policy and as frequently subservient to the curators."[3]

That museums should properly be so collection focused is by no means a matter of universal agreement. In recent years, other alternatives have been urged. In contrast with our own prevailing view of the museum as a repository, consider for instance the words that Brian Morris of the United Kingdom Museums and Galleries Commission addressed to the 1983 International Council of Museums (ICOM) triennial meeting in London:

> It is often felt that the first duty of a museum professional is to the collection he serves. He must improve it, conserve it, display it and interpret it, and his skill and training must be deployed primarily toward that end. But I say . . . it is not so. You must, of course, take the best possible care of your collection, but you must do so in order to inspire those who visit your museums . . . It is to their minds, their hearts, their imagination that you are primarily responsible. All the objects in your museum, be they never so rare, never so precious, are not more important than one single human life among those who come to see your treasures.[4]

For even a broader view, consider the opening words of the museum definition that was adopted by ICOM at its 1974 triennial meeting in Copenhagen: "A museum is a non-profitmaking, permanent institution in the service of society and its development."[5]

Or, for a still broader view, consider some of the charges and proposals made over the past few years by the Canadian-based International Movement for a New Museology (MINOM). In its critique of existing practices, it has observed that: "Many museums collect, conserve and exhibit, but they remain serparate from the present economic, social and cultural context, avoiding the mission of participating in the development of the societies they serve."[6]

With reference to MINOM's own program, in its 1984 *Declaration of Quebec* it declared that:

museology must seek to extend its traditional roles and functions of identification, conservation and education to initiatives that are more far reaching. . . . While preserving the material achievements of past civilizations and protecting the achievements characteristic of the aspirations and technology of today the new museology . . . is primarily concerned with human development, reflecting the driving forces in social progress and associating them in its plans for the future.[7]

Or consider, finally, the very direct question that Sanford Sivitz Shaman and Dr. Madhu Prakash of the Pennsylvania State University asked: "Does the museum community take seriously its responsibility for developing a responsible public that will help create a better, healthier, and ultimately safer world?"[8] Taking, then, as our starting point that it is at least arguable that the greater value of a museum's collection might lie not in its ownership and care but in its employment for socially worthwhile purposes, let us now meditate about the respective strengths of small and large museums.

II

An old proverb—John Heywood included it in his 1546 compilation of "all the proverbs in the English tongue" and Geoffrey Chaucer quoted it more than a century earlier in his *Canterbury Tales*—says that "Many small make a great."

While this may be true of some things—the billion pennies that can be aggregated together to equal $10,000,000 or the countless drops of water that together constitute the sea—it is emphatically not true of museums. In the case of museums, big is not just more little and little is not just a smaller version of big. A big museum is no more the equivalent of a cluster of small museums added together than is a small museum the equivalent of a slice removed from a big one. Put otherwise, museums are not like a set of Russian dolls, nested one inside another and all alike except for their scale. Wholly aside from scale, small and large museums differ in a number of ways.

For this discussion, at least two of these differences are important. The first is fairly obvious and will be familiar to anybody who ever worked for or with a large organization. It has to do with the seemingly unavoidable interplay between organizational scale and the growth of bureaucracy. A classic description of this linkage can be found in E. F. Schumacher's 1975 book *Small is Beautiful: Economics As If People Mattered.* Within any ongoing organization, says Schumacher, there must co-exist both an element of order and stability as well as an element that is free and creative. The relationship between these elements, however, is not a constant. Their relative strengths tend to change as the organization itself changes in scale.

Consider what happens as an organization grows. The lines of internal communication become extended. New layers of management are added. Procedures must be devised to assure the consistent treatment of recurring situations. Written instructions and reports come to take the place of face-to-face communication. Finally, at some point, more energy is required to retain control and maintain internal regularity than can be devoted to stimulating spontaneity and original thought. A bureaucracy is born. We have all seen this process occur and some of us, even, have been participants in it.

Is this inevitable? Can the elephant learn to tango? In an effort to recapture the freshness and vitality that increases of scale tend to smother, managers of large organizations have tried any number of devices. In their 1982 book *In Search of Excellence,* for example, Thomas Peters and Robert Waterman describe the effort to establish so-called "skunk works"—off-premise facilities where small teams of employees could pursue research and development work with little or no supervision, without the pressure of deadlines and free to wander in whatever ways their imaginations might prompt.[9] Other organizational theorists, though, have doubted if such groups—embedded as they are in, and funded through, a formal corporate culture—can truly have the autonomy and creativity of the spunky, upstart entrepreneurial groups they are intended to imitate. Like it or not, large organizations, whether they be museums or otherwise, may simply and inescapably be more muscle-bound than their smaller counterparts.

The second important difference attributable to scale, however, would appear to be wholly specific to museums, and considerably less evident. It has to do with the relative importance of collections to a museum's overall exhibition program. According to my own very informal survey, which may be statistically flawed but seems to me intuitively correct, the greater a museum's total gallery space, the greater also will be the proportion of that space devoted to the display of the museum's own permanent collection. The following figures may suggest just how extreme this difference can be in large and small museums.

In museums with two hundred thousand or more square feet of gallery space, the percentage of this space used to display the permanent collection consistently appears to be over 90 percent. At the Metropolitan Museum of Art, it is roughly 578 thousand out of 616 thousand square feet of total gallery space—or 94 percent. At the Natural History Museum of Los Angeles County it is 230 thousand out of 250 thousand—or 92 percent. At the Detroit Institute of Arts, it is 247 thousand out of 260 thousand—or 95 percent. At the American Museum of Natural History it is 345 thousand out of 380 thousand—or 91 percent. At the Field Museum of Natural History it is 296 thousand out of 315 thousand—or 94 percent.

At the other end of the spectrum, I found institutions such as the Fisher Gallery at the University of Southern California and the Cooper-Hewitt Museum in New York reporting that no gallery space at all was consistently set aside to display their permanent collections. In somewhat larger museums, such space still represented no more than 50 to 60 percent of the total. In Portland, Oregon, for example, the Portland Art Museum uses 13,410 out of 23,460 square feet to display its permanent collection—or 57 percent. The Oregon Historical Society uses 7,392 out of 14,317—or 52 percent. Figures from other medium-sized museums were consistent with these.

What do these numbers suggest? Two things, I think—and, again, while one is fairly obvious the other may be perhaps less so. The obvious point is that the pressure that most frequently causes a large museum to be large—large, that is, in terms of its budget, its staff, and its physical facilities—is the magnitude of its collection. It is collections, not programs, that generally power the growth of museums.

The less obvious point is based upon the assumption that there is some similarity—not necessarily a perfect correlation, but at least some similarity—between how a museum allocates its available gallery space and how it allocates the other programmatic resources that it has available. The point itself is this: that the overall program of a large museum will, in general, tend to be more closely tied to its own permanent collection than will be the program of a smaller one. Given what we know about the burden of caring for a large collection—and what we know, as well, about the inevitably bureaucratic tendencies of the necessarily larger organization needed to care for such a large collection— we may also expect that, more often than not, such a program will be relatively static in comparison to the program that a smaller museum—not so heavily burdened by a large collection and far more flexible in its management—might be able to present.

If such an analysis is correct, then what we must recognize is how the respective strengths and weaknesses of small and large museums appear to complement one another in an almost natural way. The very magnitude of the collection that makes a large museum large may also disable it from practicing the program flexibility that a smaller museum might enjoy. Conversely, the very desire to maintain such flexibility might disable the smaller museum from ever undertaking a more vigorous course of collections acquisitions and care. Need these differences be leveled out? Should we strive to make small and large museums more like one another? Does the official rhetoric of our field require that we at least urge small museums to make the acquisition and care of collections a more central concern? Or can we—as a field—

take advantage of the different strengths of small and large museums to further increase what museums are able to contribute to—in the words of the ICOM definition—"the service of society and its development"? It is this latter alternative, I will argue, that offers us the richer possibilities.

III

In a recent issue of *ICOM News* the French museologist Robert Julien called for the greater politicalization of museums—not meaning that they should participate in partisan politics but rather that they should be engaging themselves more deeply with those larger public issues that vitally affect the lives of their communities, their countries, or even the future of humankind. Specific to Dr. Julien's comments were environmental and ecological issues and the need he saw for natural history museums to address these in greater depth.[10]

In a similar vein, Alice Carnes of the Willamette Science and Technology Center in Oregon has written eloquently of the need for science museums to provide a forum through which the public can explore the ethical and public policy issues that are raised by advances in science and technology.[11] In all deference to their comments, I would nonetheless submit that the degree to which natural history and science museums have been able to bring these environmental, ecological, and technological issues into focus for their visitors is already far in advance of what museums of other disciplines have been willing or able to do with respect to the many remaining problems of this deeply troubled century.

The arms race still proceeds at ever more lethal levels. Atomic weapons proliferate. Homelessness spreads in our cities. Terrorism encroaches upon diplomacy. Art is converted to a commodity. Religion is infected by chicanery. Racism remains a reality. We neither know how to deal with dope, nor how to cope with AIDS, nor how to moderate the growing disparity between poverty and wealth. So inadequate are our mechanisms to alleviate suffering that thousands of children die wholly unnecessary deaths every single day. Throughout much of the world, individual liberties are brushed aside by the asserted needs of the state. Throughout much of the world, ethnic and religious groups that once were submerged in the culture of others now struggle— often with arms—to discover identities of their own.

Is there nothing that museums can do to help society address these issues? Is the creation of—in Mr. Shaman's and Dr. Prakash's phrase—"a better, healthier, and ultimately safer world" something which is so wholly beyond our interests or ability that we need not even consider it as a possibility? Are those of us who work in museums really fit to do little more than take periodic inventories, maintain our climate controls, and roll back an occasional outbreak of bronze disease? Is it that we lack the will or the means to deal more directly with the overarching issues of our time? Or is it that what we truly lack is a conception or a theory or a vision of the museum and its potential that would permit it—or even encourage it—to participate more fully in what Justice Holmes called the "passion and action of [its] time"?

And yet, if museums truly are to be "in the service of society and its development," if the worthwhile use of collections—not merely their accumulation and care—is to be the basis on which both museums and we who work in them are to claim some public importance, then it seems to me that we have little choice but, at the very least, to explore whether and how museums can help their visitors address these and kindred issues. The stakes are too great not at least to try.

But how are we to do this? Would the exhibition formats that we currently use be sufficient to deal with a more abstract range of issues? Could we produce balanced presentations that would stimulate our visitors rather than biased ones that might only serve to indoctrinate them? Could we carry out such a program, and still retain our credibility? On a more basic level: Who would decide what is socially worthwhile? When we dealt with topics that may be highly controversial, how would we reconcile what might be different points of view both within and between a museum's governing body and its staff? Would our present structures of governance be adequate to such a situation?

Is a call for social action even compatible with a museum system that is in so large a part privately governed and funded? Would traditional funding sources underwrite such programs? What alternative patterns of support and accountability might be required?

Speaking in 1974 at ICOM's tenth triennial, Lennart Holm—then Chairman of Denmark's State Commission for Museums and Exhibitions—acknowledged how difficult such an involvement might be, particularly when compared with the ability of natural history museums to deal with environmental and ecological issues from what he termed a purely "scientific" viewpoint.

> The shortcomings of society, the imbalance of economic distribution, [and] intellectual and political dishonesty cannot be demonstrated with the same statistical certainty and the same categorical reference to laws of nature as ecological changes. Museum documentation of social conditions is always liable to be considered more subjective, more maliciously aimed at the criticism of existing institutions and persons and, of course, is more often subject to the attentions and attempted influence of critical factions."[12]

How, then, are we to deal with such difficulties? At this point, none of us really knows. In our national and regional meetings we have been far more apt to focus on problems of technique than on these problems of purpose. The same has been largely true of our official publications. Beyond that, it is by no means clear that we can find the answers by theorizing. We may only be able to do so through experiment, by trial and error. And it is precisely here, I think, that the small museum might be uniquely structured to play a leading experimental role in helping us to explore whether this museum field of ours can move itself at least a little way toward being—I take the phrases from Dr. Peter van Mensch, the Dutch museum commentator—somewhat less "object centered" and somewhat more "community centered."

In assigning purposes to our museums, there is nothing that obligates us to follow any particular model. Museums are our own human creation—neither based on any changeless ideal nor occurring as a fact of nature—and they are a creation that we are free to shape and reshape as may best suit our needs. In giving museums their shape, it is not even required that we confine ourselves to a single shape. Rich possibilities, for example, might lie in designing different museums for different purposes with the intent that they ultimately operate in collaboration rather than entirely on their own. Might not just such a collaboration between small and large museums—a collaboration in which they each retained their currently different strengths and weaknesses—be precisely the means through which we could move this field to a somewhat more "community-centered" position than it occupies today?

What if, rather than making it our goal that each and every museum must collect and preserve and utilize, we were to agree that some, the large ones, were to emphasize their roles in collection and preservation, while others, the small ones, were to concentrate on utilization? To over-simplify badly: large museums could be object centered. We would expect them to serve as the principal repositories and caretakers of our material heritage, to provide smaller museums with expanded conservation and other technical services, and to be the primary source of loans. Small museums could be community centered. They, in turn, would concentrate on presenting special exhibitions and other programs that drew on the collection resources of the larger museums and addressed the aesthetic, historic, political, and scientific issues relevant to their communities. With each size of institution specializing in what it did best, such a symbiotic approach might assure that the musuem field as a whole—rather than each entity within it—could maximize its ability to acquire, maintain, and utilize collections "in the service of society and its development" and to contribute toward "a better, healthier and ultimately safer world."

For such a collaborative undertaking to work, there would be several requirements. One, of course, would be funding. For some time, the kind of special exhibition funds that regularly go to larger museums would have to be diverted—at least in part—so that smaller museums could mount a more ambitious range of presentations. As much or more important, however, would be a change in expectation: an understanding that a small art museum, for example, should not try to become a miniature Metropolitan Museum of Art—something it is only bound to do badly—but should instead become an exemplary center for exhibitions and related public programming. Its principal goal ought not be to acquire and maintain collections but rather to stimulate its community in important ways by making the most imaginative use possible of the collections that others have acquired and maintained. For large museums, the converse might be true. Our principal expectations of these might revolve around the increase and maintenance of their collections, around their research activities, and around their active and continuing support of the smaller institutions that can work more directly and flexibly with the community.

The notion that all museums need not be alike and that we might legitimately have different expectations of institutions of different scales should not be a shocking one. We do not expect an experimental theater group to mount the same plays as a Broadway producer or a small regional press to publish materials of the same sort as a Madison Avenue publisher. The distinction is not merely one of nonprofit versus profit; it is also one of small against large. We certainly do not expect the Navy to design a PT boat to function like a miniature battleship or a Chihuahua to slog through the snow like a St. Bernard. Why, then, should a similar distinction between small and large museums not be equally legitimate?

The foregoing, of course, is subject to enormous qualification. The situation of a small museum in a community already well furnished with large museums is clearly different from that of a small museum that may be the only institution of its discipline within two hundred miles. The situation of a small museum created out of specific historical conditions is clearly different from one that was not. Not considered at all here has been the situation of the middle-sized museum, which might still have to maintain some balance between object centeredness and community centeredness.

Nonetheless, the conclusion of my own meditation on small and large museums is that we do our field a tremendous disservice when we fail to recognize, first, that small and large museums tend to have different strengths and weaknesses, and second, that at this historical moment it is the particular strength of the small museum—likely to be more flexible in its management and less burdened by the weight of a large collection—that might be uniquely important in moving the American museum community toward a more socially relevant role than its official object centeredness currently permits it to play. For those of us who think that some movement in this direction is important, the small museum may well be our very best hope.

Notes

1. *Museums for a New Century* (Washington, D.C.: American Association of Museums, 1984), 34–35.

2. Paul Di Maggio, *Managers of the Arts,* NEA Research Division Report No. 20 (Washington, D.C.: National Endowment for the Arts, September 1987), 21.

3. Elliot W. Eisner and Stephen M. Dobbs, *The Uncertain Profession: Observations on the State of Museum Education in Twenty American Art Museums* (Los Angeles: Getty Center for Education in the Arts, Spring 1986), 20.

4. Brian Morris, *Proceedings of the Tenth ICOM Triennial Meeting, London, 1983* (London: ICOM, 1984), 15.

5. International Council of Museums, *Statutes: Code of Professional Ethics* (Paris: ICOM, 1987), 3.

6. MINOM Communique, Lisbon, 1985.

7. "Declaration of Quebec: Basic Principles for a New Museology," *Museum* 148 (1985): 201.

8. Sanford Sivitz Shaman and Dr. Madhu Prakash, "Long Range Planning for Museums: Promoting Public Escapism or Education for Public Responsibility," *The Museologist* 51 (No. 17b, Summer 1987): 11.

9. Thomas J. Peters and Robert H. Waterman Jr., *In Search of Excellence: Lessons from America's Best-Run Companies* (Cambridge: Harper & Row, 1982), 201.

10. *ICOM News* 40 (No. 1, 1987): 6.

11. Alice Carnes, "Showplace, Playground, or Forum? Choice Point for Science Museums," *Museum News* 64 (April 1986): 29–35.

12. Lennart Holm, *Proceedings of the Tenth ICOM Triennial Meeting, 67.*

THE PROPER BUSINESS
OF THE MUSEUM: IDEAS
OR THINGS?

To begin, let me ask you to imagine a new museum—heavily endowed, well situated in a prime downtown area, installed in its own large, modern and climate-controlled building, and devoted wholly and exclusively to the collection, preservation, study, interpretation, and display of toothpicks.

The National Toothpick Museum—or the NTM as it's more commonly known—is multidisciplinary. In the Hall of Oral Hygiene, for example, elementary school children learn about the toothpick's role as a humble foot soldier in the neverending struggle against tooth decay and gum disease. In the Hall of History, visitors can see *Pick the Winner,* an exhibition of toothpicks used by successful politicians and other high achievers. Elsewhere are toothpicks associated with great historic events—those chewed by Roosevelt, Churchill and Stalin at Yalta, for example, or by Reagan and Gorbachev at their summit in Moscow. Nearby are the first three toothpicks sent into space and also a selection of toothpicks used by movie stars. The Rudolph Valentino specimen has proven to be a particular favorite.

Beyond this, the NTM also maintains a full program of

changing exhibitions, regularly offers symposia and lectures, and publishes a quarterly journal, *History's Splendid Splinter,* which carries scholarly articles about the toothpick's role in social history, patterns of forestry, and the evolving technology of toothpick manufacture.

Virtually nobody ever visits the NTM, nor does the press frequently write about it. This, however, does not disturb its director. As he commented with some hauteur during a recent interview: "Here at the NTM we stick pretty close to our mission statement. Our collections are in splendid shape, our records are complete and up to date and our scholarship is considered impeccable. We're attempting to run a first-rate, responsible museum—not trying to win a popularity contest."

What are we to think of this toothpick museum? Shall we permit it to be perpetuated? Ought we, directly or indirectly, give it our public support? Shall we admit it to our museum associations? Will we welcome its curators as our colleagues?

Our common sense tells us that this is a ridiculous endeavor, a venture that might be acceptable enough as a hobby but which becomes grotesque and preposterous when inflated to the level of a large-scale museum.

Curiously enough, however, if we approach the NTM not in this commonsense way but through the conventional wisdom of the museum field, then it can begin to assume a certain, plausible legitimacy. That this should be so is the outcome of three separate but nonetheless connected developments that we have seen occurring in many museums over the past two decades.

These are, first: a tendency to consider museums in the light of their functional definition rather than in terms of their purposes; second, the assertion that it is the collection and care of objects that lies at the heart of the museum enterprise; and third, the extraordinary technical proficiency that we have developed in the care of objects and in their display, whether as parts of our permanent collections or within the context of special exhibitions.

That museums should be commonly defined in functional rather than purposive terms is not surprising. The very utility of a definition is to clarify what is different and distinctive about the subject it defines. What is different and distinctive about museums, of course, is that they collect and display objects. That they do so for a larger and publicly beneficial purpose—a purpose that they may to a degree share with a community's schools, hospitals, churches, symphony orchestras and day-care facilities—is neither different nor distinctive. Ergo, that museums at bottom *do* have a larger and a publicly beneficial purpose is not a characteristic that often appears in their definition.

One turns to the common dictionary definition of a museum as "a room, building or locale where a collection of objects is put on exhibition" and the NTM appears well enough qualified. Nor does it fare much worse when one looks, at least superficially, at the definition used for accreditation purposes by the American Association of Museums (AAM):

> an organized and permanent non-profit institution, essentially educational or esthetic in purpose, with professional staff, which owns and utilizes tangible objects, cares for them and exhibits them to the public on some regular schedule.

Not only does the NTM seem just fine—assuming it employs a curator, a conservator or at least an educator, it even seems accreditable.

Turning to a Canadian definition of museums—my source is the 1981 statement prepared by the National Museums of Canada for the Federal Cultural Policy Review Committee—one finds this:

> Museums collect, they preserve and study what they collect and they share both the collections and the knowledge derived therefrom for the instruction and self-enlightenment of an audience.

Again, we can perhaps welcome the NTM to our ranks.

Even if one turns to that most socially oriented of all museum definitions, the one which the International Council of Museums adopted in 1974, the NTM still seems to retain its legitimacy.

A museum is a non-profitmaking, permanent institution in the service of society and of its development, and open to the public, which acquires, conserves, researches, communicates and exhibits, for purposes of study, education and enjoyment, material evidence of man and his environment.

While some might question to what degree a toothpick museum may be in the service of society and its development, certainly nobody—or at least nobody who ever had a kernel of corn stuck in his teeth—would ever argue that the celebration of this humble but useful implement was a *disservice* to society and its development. From a functional perspective, the NTM still seems to be a museum.

There are, I think, at least two reasons why this functional perspective has taken so strong a grip. For one thing, it has proven comfortable. To focus museum rhetoric on the socially beneficial aspects of a museum would ultimately be to invite discussion on a wide range of political and moral issues that could well pit trustees against staff members and staff members against one another. By contrast, to focus on function—on the good, seemingly value-free work of collecting, preserving and displaying—projects a sense of ideological neutrality (albeit, I suspect, a grossly deceptive sense) in which people of diverse social views are able to work more amiably together.

Beyond that, this functional perspective connects with our aspirations towards professionalism. Among the key elements needed to establish museum work—or any other occupation—as a separate and distinct profession is the ability to identify some aspect of that work as being unique. This process is, in a way, parallel to the way definitions are constructed. We tend to build these around what is most distinctive, not necessarily what is most important. Motive, impulse, and purpose are sheared away leaving us simply to function as professional collectors, pre-servers and exhibitors.

Not surprisingly, a similar reductive tendency is reflected, and even reinforced, by our larger professional museum associations. These derive their strength from what is common among their membership, not what is diverse. What's most common, of course, is how their members—diverse as they may be in discipline—all function as custodians, scholars, and public inter-preters. Frequently, then, these are the aspects of museum work to which our associations give the most stress. There is no harm in this if we understand the context and the limited nature of such an emphasis. There may, however, be great harm when we lose sight of this context and begin to mistake what we do—that is collecting, preserving and displaying—for our raison d'être. That's when something as silly as a museum wholly devoted to toothpicks can begin to seem plausible and legitimate.

When we turn to the assertion that objects and their care—whether these be works of art, historic artifacts, or natural his-tory specimens—lie at the heart of the museum enterprise, we encounter a similar group of considerations. This is, for one thing, a comfortable assertion. It tends to finesse the philosophic and ideological controversies with which we might otherwise have to contend if we recognized that concepts and relationships, and not things alone, lie equally at the heart of museum work. For another, it offers a further basis on which to build our larger professional associations. The assumption that we are all doing fundamentally the same thing—i.e., dealing with objects—not only serves as the glue to hold these together but also acts to support a growing literature and even a burgeoning array of museum studies programs.

Again, though, we must be careful. Intertwined with this assertion is the belief—by no means universal, but held broadly enough to be significant—that objects have (and the pun here is deliberate) some "objective" reality—that a museum object can, with only the most minimal help, in some way speak for itself. Allied with this is a notion of the museum as a sort of neutral and transparent medium—a clear, clean, and undistorting lens— through which the public ought be able to come face-to-face with an object, pure and fresh.

At best, this seems a willful naïveté. The world, as William James has taught us, is not something that we can grasp perceptually. Taken as a whole, it is—in his grand phrase—"a big, blooming, buzzing confusion." It is only through selective attention and the formulation of concepts that we are able to reduce this blooming confusion to some comprehensible form. These are matters of the mind, the consequences of thought. For us, objects do not exist alone. We perceive them in a mesh of experience. Whether in a museum or otherwise, objects only have meaning for us through the framework of the concepts and assumptions with which we approach them. We see things, as the anthropologist David Pilbeam has observed, not as they are but "as we are."

If this is so, then we must never forget that ideas—and not just things alone—also lie at the heart of the museum enterprise. Reality is neither objects alone nor simply ideas about objects but, rather, the two taken together. Of percepts and concepts, James wrote: "We need them both, as we need both our legs to walk with."

Too often, though, this thought component remains unarticulated; it remains in the realm of the taken-for-granted. If museums were nothing more than custodial agents, this might not matter. Nor might it matter if museums were simply centers for scholarship. But if museums are to serve some greater beneficial purpose—if museums are to have some real and powerful impact on the lives of those who use them—then it matters a great deal. Unless we can understand the intellectual framework through which we perceive an object, and unless we more fully understand the various intellectual frameworks through which the members of our public might themselves in turn perceive that same object, how can we ever truly hope to be in communication?

In the case of the NTM, our toothpick museum, the third of these three recent developments in museums—the enormous growth in our technical proficiency—seems particularly germane. The issue is one of technology.

Until the twentieth century, the term "technology" was generally used only with respect to the practical or industrial applications of scientific principles. It referred, for the most part, to the use of tools and machinery. In our own time, though, it has taken on a broader meaning. We use it today to cover all of the systematic means and processes by which we accomplish our various tasks. In his 1954 book *La Technique,* Jacques Ellul referred to these as "the ensemble of practices by which one uses available resources in order to achieve certain valued ends."

Viewed in that light, museum work can be considered a technology, of which we who work in museums have indeed become the very skilled masters and mistresses. Along with that bright recognition, however, there must come another and a darker one: that technology is not merely a neutral or inert means by which we are able to pursue our traditional goals. It can also have an insidious side-effect. This is a condition—the phrase was most recently used by Garry Wills, but the possibility was long ago recognized by Ellul—that might be called "technological determinancy."

Put in everyday terms, "technological determinancy" means that we may find ourselves doing things simply because we know how to do them, regardless of whether they truly satisfy any real desire. Put in museum-relevant terms, it means that the "ensemble of practices" that we have developed permits us to sometimes perform the most dazzling museological feats simply because we can, and not because the outcome necessarily fulfills any legitimate purpose or meets any genuine need. As museum people, we have become so technically proficient, so ingenious in what we do, that we are capable of developing a perfectly plausible museological program to meet virtually any challenge—even devising and maintaining a museum to glorify the toothpick.

How might this be different? How might we conceive of museums in such a way that the NTM would be a palpable absurdity from its very inception? To begin with, we must resist the siren song of technology. Also, we must better understand that the museum is a place for both objects and ideas. Above all, though, we must begin to shift our focus—and the focuses of those who supervise and support us—from function to purpose. We must start with the proposition that the museum's raison d'être is to provide an important public benefit, to have an important impact on the lives of others—not merely to provide a custodial or a scholarly service—and we must then proceed to inqure into what the nature of that benefit and that impact might be.

Throughout, though, we must also pause from time to time to reflect upon the caution of William Blake: "To Generalize is to be an Idiot. To Particularize is the Alone Distinction of Merit." The public benefit and impact that a museum can provide will never be the same in any two institutions. The real guts and glory of every museum is in its particularity, not in what it does in common with others. As museums vary enormously by discipline, collections, scale, facilities, context, location, funding, and history, so too must the mix of benefits they can provide be varied from institution to institution. What we can generalize about, though, are some of the elements that might be included in that mix—some of the different ways in which museums might contribute to the better lives of those who use them.

As traditionally conceived, of course, museums may serve as important providers of information. In the rhetoric of the museum as educational institution, this role has generally been given a principal stress. While museums have always been informative, is the museum still an important medium for the dissemination of information? Less so, I suspect, than might once have been the case. Such media as radio, broadcast television and the videocassette recorder may have come to serve at least as effectively as exhibits to disseminate information about certain subjects that once were the exclusive province of museums.

There is, though, a further difficulty. Common both to museums and to these more recently evolved media is a troubling question about the information that they disseminate. Is this information as objective as we once believed it to be? To an extent not hitherto suspected, we must face the possibility that, despite all our goodwill, the assumptions and biases that color our larger social and political views may also color our simplest and most basic acts of identification and classification. As the University of Chicago's Neil Harris pointed out when he addressed the AAM's Midwest Museum Conference in September 1986, " . . . classification has come to be seen as an act of domination as well as analysis." As for the traditional authority of museums, he said: "The museum's voice is no longer seen as transcendent. Rather it is implicated in the distribution of wealth, power, knowledge, and taste shaped by the larger social order."

Suffice it to say that however we elect to respond to that charge, it will have to be in terms of ideas, not of objects.

What if, instead, we looked not at information but at values? The notion of the museum as a disseminator of values is a complex one. In the mix of what museums provide to the public, this has long been one of their most significant, and at the same time most controversial roles. On the one hand, we are urged to maintain the art museum as the last bastion of esthetic standards in a world of rising visual mediocrity. On the other, we are cautioned about how easily the history museum can be used— the phrase comes from Felipe Lacouture of the National Museum of History of Mexico—as "an ideological tool of the State." Particularly tricky is the fact that what may seem wholly objective to one observer may seem just the opposite to another. Those of us at the Smithsonian Institution who naively believed that our own National Museum of Natural History was a value-neutral institution were certainly astonished several years ago when a group of religious creationists brought a legal action in an effort—unsuccessful as it turned out—to redress what they considered a value-driven and not scientifically based exhibit about human evolution.

If what we take to be factual information is as Neil Harris said, "shaped by the larger social order," is this not even more so in the case of our values? Can we even distinguish what we ourselves believe from the spirit of our time as it finds individual expression through each of us?

Discussing nineteenth-century British municipal museums, the American historian David Lowenthal has most succinctly described them as "aimed to instill moral thinking and behavior: built in the image of classical temples and Gothic churches, (they) served the masses as intimidating reminders of ruling class power and their own ignorance."

Did the men who built those museums intend them that way? If not, might they nonetheless have been proud of what they succeeded in projecting? Do we really know what values our own museums project? Or will a century's distance be needed to make that clear?

The issue, certainly, is not one of having value-free museums. Few of us would want this; many of us who work in museums do so with a certain missionary zeal. We do so with a passionate belief in the importance of our subject matter and, not infrequently, with a profound commitment to what we believe to be the underlying values of that subject matter.

The real issue is not how to purge the museum of values, in all likelihood an impossible task, but how to make those values manifest, how to bring them up to consciousness for both ourselves and our visitors. We delude ourselves when we think of the museum as a clear and transparent medium through which only our objects transmit messages. We transmit messages too—as a medium we are also a message—and it seems to me vital that we understand better just what those messages are.

An alternate approach would be to consider the museum primarily as a medium by which to provide visitors with an extraordinary experience—a place in which they might directly encounter rare and/or costly objects not generally a part of their everyday lives. As one proponent of this view—Father M. A.

Couturier, the young Dominican who once persuaded Henri Matisse to decorate the chapel in Venice—phrased it, "A museum should be a place where we lose our head—to be enlightened, dazzled and transformed by the epiphany of art."

Here, though, another caution might be in order. We ought not to claim too much. While most of us at one time or another have experienced the dazzle, enlightenment, and transformation of encountering a great object, the fact is that there are by no means nearly enough epiphanous works of art or wonders of nature to fill the thousands upon thousands of museums that stand on this continent alone.

It seems to me a serious disservice to the public to raise an expectation that museum-going may provide a transcendent experience in those situations when none is reasonably to be expected. What happens when we show less than the best works of art, for example, as if these were masterworks? At best, a visitor may fault us for our inadequacy. At worst, he may fault himself for having failed to respond. The better way, of course, is to be candid. That, again, suggests that we must bring thought into some closer parity with things and make a discussion of ideas—not just a display of objects—an integral part of the visitor's museum-going experience.

Beyond information, values, and experience, what else of social utility might museums provide to their public? Let me suggest two: stimulation and empowerment. Here we approach the museum visit not as an end in itself but as the starting point, rather, for a process intended to continue long after the visitor has left the museum's premises.

In the United States, the roots of this approach can be traced back to John Cotton Dana, the early-twentieth-century Yankee iconoclast who bitterly dismissed most of the country's then newly palatial museums as "awesome to a few, tiresome to many, and helpful to almost none." In his 1917 book *The New Museum,* Dana urged that the museums of the future make a special effort to attract the young and to interest them in making collections of their own—collections that they might ultimately share with the public. This development of the collecting habit, he wrote:

> with its accompanying education of powers of observation, its training in handwork, its tendency to arouse interests theretofore unsuspected even by those who possess them, its continuous suggestions toward good taste and refinement which lie in the process of installing even the most modest of collections, and its leanings toward sound civic interest through doing for one's community a helpful thing—this work of securing the co-operation of boys and girls, making them useful while they are gaining their own pleasure and carrying on their own education, is one of the coming museum's most promising fields.

In recent years, perhaps nobody has put the argument for the museum as a source of stimulation more powerfully than did Nelson Goodman of Harvard when the CMA and the AAM met jointly in Boston in 1980. Speaking initially of works of art, he said:

> The museum has to function as an institution for the prevention of blindness in order to make works work. And making works work is the museum's major mission.
>
> Works work when, by stimulating inquisitive looking, sharpening perception, raising visual intelligence, widening perspectives, bringing out new connections and contrasts, and marking off neglected significant kinds, they participate in the organization and reorganization of experience, in the making and remaking of our worlds.

Carrying his observation beyond works of art, Goodman continued:

> Clearly, works of science work in this sense, too, and so also do the collections of science museums, historical museums, and botanical and zoological gardens. . . . Museums of different kinds indeed

have some different problems, but their common end is improvement in the comprehension and creation of the worlds we live in.

To the extent that we want such stimulation to be in the mix of what a museum provides, how might it affect what we choose to display and how we choose to display it? What criterion should guide such a decision: the inherent quality of an object or its utility as a stimulus? Or are these the same thing? Here, again, we are beyond any functional view of the museum. However we choose to answer such questions, we will have to begin in the realm of thought, and not collections management.

Closely related to this view of the museum as stimulus is the vision of the museum as an instrument of empowerment. Its goal as such would be to provide the members of its public with a knowledge of the methods, processes, and techniques through which they, in turn, could make better-informed judgments about their own past and more insightful choices about their future. The museum would not presume to teach a subject but would provide the means by which its clients could learn the subject for themselves. Rather than holding itself forth as the authoritative or exclusive source of historical interpretation or aesthetic judgment, the museum would hope to enlist the visitor as a collaborator who might, in turn, develop his own sense of heritage, causality, connectedness, and taste—his own links to both an individual and a communal past.

This two-way approach, of course, is chiefly characteristic of the eco-museum movement and has most recently been embraced within the program of the Committee for a New Museology. As summarized at the October 1987, International Workshop on New Museology held in Aragon, Spain, it proposes a museology that:

> must be defined according to changing social realities rather than to a theory forced upon populations; methodologies should be based on specific social realities and should aim for the liberation,

development and transformation of society through the awareness and participation of the population.

What the New Museology will be able to accomplish remains to be seen. Whatever it is, though, it should certainly be something more significant than that imaginary accomplishment of the old museology—a toothpick museum.

Those, then, are some of the possibilities open to us if we are to envision our museums as fundamentally driven-by-purpose rather than devoted-to-objects. For each of us, the best mix of those possibilities will be different. Common to all, however, should be the notion that the primary and central relationship of museology is between the museum and its visitors and other clients—not between the museum and its collection. Common as well should be the sense that it is ideas, viewpoint, and insight that finally powers the museum—not the care of collections. Good collections management is essential, but it can no more make a museum excellent than good bookkeeping can make a business flourish.

The question we must ultimately ask ourselves is this: do our museums make a real difference in, and do they have a positive impact on, the lives of other people. If not, if in the end we are only the servants of our collections and not of our fellow humans, then we might just as well be off someplace plying our trades at some imaginary Temple of Thumbtacks, Paper Clip Palace, or even the NTM. But if so, if the life of the community is richer for the work we do, if we make an important and positive difference in the lives of others, then the zeal we bring to our daily work will have been well rewarded, and our own working lives well spent.

RETHINKING THE MUSEUM

An Emerging New Paradigm

It was nearly twenty years ago, in the April
1970 issue of *Museum News*, that Joseph
Veach Noble—later to serve as a distinguished president of the
American Association of Museums—published his "Museum
Manifesto." In it, Noble briefly described what he took to be the
five basic responsibilities of every museum: to *collect*, to *conserve*, to *study*, to *interpret*, and to *exhibit*. Stressed as well was
the interrelationship among these responsibilities. "[T]hey
form," he said, "an entity. They are like the five fingers of a hand,
each independent but united for common purpose. If a museum
omits or slights any of these five responsibilities, it has hand-
icapped itself immeasurably."

During the two decades since, Noble's five-part analysis of
museum functions has proven enormously useful. As an evalua-
tive tool, it has supplied a series of perspectives from which a
museum's performance might be systematically judged. Employed as an armature, it has provided a sturdy framework
around which to build such diverse structures as museum organizational charts, collections management policies, and the curric-
ula of various museum studies programs.

Despite its utility, however, a superseding paradigm now appears to be emerging. By no means entirely new, it amends rather than replaces Noble's 1970 formulation. In so doing, it is both prescriptive with respect to the future operation of museums and, to some degree, correspondingly questioning (if not actually critical) of certain of their recent past practices.

A version of this new paradigm was first introduced to me by Peter van Mensch, the Dutch museologist who teaches at the Reinwardt Academy in Leiden. As analyzed by van Mensch, the essential functions of museums are reduced to three: to *preserve* (to collect being viewed as simply an early step in that process), to *study* (a function that remains unchanged) and to *communicate* (this third function being a combination of Noble's final two, i.e., to interpret and to exhibit). Noteworthy is the degree to which van Mensch's analysis parallels that of John Henry Merryman of the Stanford University Law School in his recent studies of public policy with respect to cultural property. The basic framework of any such policy, Merryman has concluded, must be based upon "the ordered triad of preservation, truth and access."

In seeking to establish a more direct link between the museum's activities as a collecting institution and its ability to preserve what it actually collects, this amended approach closely accords with the positions most recently taken by the major professional organizations representing the field. Thus, paragraph 3.1 of the *Code of Professional Ethics* adopted by the International Council of Museums at its 1986 triennial meeting in Buenos Aires provides: "Museums should not, except in very exceptional circumstances, acquire material that the museum is unlikely to be able to catalogue, conserve, store or exhibit, as appropriate, in a proper manner."

In a similar vein is the position taken by the AAM in its 1984 report *Museums for a New Century*. In the first recommendation of that report, museums were urged to collect "carefully and purposefully." Specifically suggested was that every museum must "exercise care by collecting within its capacity to house and

preserve the objects, artifacts and specimens in its stewardship."
Earlier pronouncements did not link these activities so strongly.
Indeed, the AAM's 1925 ethics code—its first—did not address
the matter of preservation at all.

To say that a museum ought not collect artifacts and specimens for which it cannot properly care—whether because of
their inherent fragility or because the institution lacks the resources necessary to do so—has more than an ethical dimension.
It has practical implications that extend to the acquisition process itself, potentially strengthening the role of the conservation
specialist vis à vis that of the curator. The rarity, importance, or
desirability of an object may no longer be a wholly sufficient
(albeit still necessary) justification for its acquisition. Equally
basic might be the question of its future care.

Such a fusion of the question of desirability with the question of preservability might, moreover, better undergird the increasingly made demand that the proffer to a museum of a
collection object be accompanied by the proffer of the resources
required for its long-term care. Museums are, for the most part,
neither archives nor depositories of last resort. They can no
longer (if they ever could) afford to look after boundless ag-
glomerations of objects acquired for no better reason than that
they became available. The careful shaping of a collection intended for a mission-driven use requires a more considered balance between the collection that is assembled and the museum's
ability to provide that collection with a proper level of care.

Nonetheless, this perception of a tighter link between collecting and preserving—this sense that they should not, as Noble
had originally conceived of them, be considered as interrelated
functions but, rather, as different aspects of the same function—
ought not cause any too great an alteration of current museum
practices. Its implications are not nearly so far-reaching as those
of the second change that this new paradigm contemplates—the
fusion of the museum's interpretive and exhibition functions. In
place today is a widely utilized scheme of museum organization
that reflects the notion that interpretation is an activity distinct

from (and most frequently posterior to) the display of museum objects in an exhibition format. This is most evident in the existence of separate departments of museum education.

Critical to understand is that this perceived fusion of interpretation and exhibition does not arise from any sense that these functions *should* be combined. It comes, rather, from the realization that these functions are so intertwined with one another as to be inseparable. What has become compellingly clear is the extent to which—like speech, like writing, like every other form of human discourse—an exhibition is shaped from its very outset by the values, attitudes, and assumptions of those who choose and arrange the objects that it contains. Whatever the power of the explanatory materials created to surround these objects— didactic labels, gallery handouts, catalogues, recorded tours, docent talks, lectures, films, and symposia—it is the exhibition itself, and not this educational nimbus, that radiates the strongest interpretive emanations. As the late René d'Harnoncourt, then director of New York's Museum of Modern Art, observed some thirty years ago: "There is no such thing as a neutral installation."

This phenomenon has recently drawn increasing attention. Writing in the summer 1987 issue of the Canadian magazine *Muse*, Deidre Sklar, a researcher working with Native American artifacts, discussed the paradox of displaying such materials under normal museum conditions. "Time and space in a museum," she wrote, "are defined in terms of the confines of the collection, not of the context from which [the collection is] drawn. Visiting hours from ten to five and glass exhibit cases define Euro-American, not native American time and space."

In that same issue, the Canadian anthropologist Chris Miller-Marti speculated as to whether museum exhibits, regardless of the time and place with which they ostensibly deal, must not inescapably reflect the values and beliefs of contemporary society. Central to these, she suggested, were the "concepts of progress, technology, rationality and domination over nature." What museum exhibits appear to be telling us, she concluded, is "more about ourselves than our ancestors, more about our own values and concepts than those of the culture they profess to portray."

The Smithsonian Institution addressed this same issue in the fall of 1988 when it played host to an international conference— *The Poetics and Politics of Representation*—that addressed the question of whether and how one culture could appropriately present another in a museum setting. In a preliminary description of the program, the organizers described it thus:

> [We] will consider the fundamental relationship between ideas and objects, conception and presentation in the context of exhibitions. We will organize . . . around two general approaches: the poetics and politics of representation. Poetics, in this case, may be understood as identifying the underlying narrative/aesthetic patterns within exhibitions. The politics of representation refers to the social circumstances in which exhibitions are organized, presented, and understood. Clearly, these are intersecting domains which draw on a common pool of historical memory and shared (often unconscious) assumption.

As in anthropology, so in art. A workshop presented at the February 1989 conference of the College Art Association dealt with nineteenth-century American landscape painting and challenged the adequacy of how such works were generally exhibited. Specifically raised was the question of how museums "might find modes of installation and exhibition which illuminate more effectively the multivalent significance of images and the complexity of their ideological function as forms of cultural expressiveness."

This increasing recognition of the inseparability of the museum's interpretive and exhibition functions raises a host of important questions. Should museum education appropriately remain the responsibility of a separate department? If so, should that department—as distinct from a curatorial department— also be principally responsible for the organization of exhibitions? In either event, to what extent are museum workers able to articulate for themselves the values, attitudes, and assumptions that underlie the exhibitions they now organize? To what degree can or ought those values, attitudes, and assumptions be articulated to the visiting public as well? Must those values, attitudes, and assumptions always be considered as "givens," or might they sometimes (and, if so, when and by whose initiative) require some modification?

A further question—possibly even more important—concerns the scope of the interactions and experiences that we might envision this combined interpretive-exhibition function as embracing. Do we currently have available a single term that does full justice to the full range of these? So far as it goes, "communication"—the description proposed by van Mensch—has several distinct advantages. For one thing, it would be consonant with many of the most fundamental goals that museums have characterized themselves as pursuing, especially with respect to the education of their visitors. These goals—in a mix that varies widely from museum to museum—would certainly include: to provide access, to disseminate information, to instruct, to illuminate and clarify historic or contemporary situations and relationships, to set standards, to introduce and strengthen cultural values, to elevate taste, to pose issues, to develop skills, to offer a sense of empowerment, to establish and promote social identity and—in the most extreme instances—to inculcate and to persuade.

A second advantage of van Mensch's description is the ease with which it would permit some simple model of linear communication to be used as a tool to measure a museum's effectiveness. If we conceive of the museum fundamentally as a formulator and broadcaster of messages, then it ought be a relatively simple task to evaluate the success of its operations. Exactly what messages is the museum seeking to transmit? Is it able to formulate and transmit those messages in a manner that is consistently free of static, distortion, and interference? Are those messages being clearly received by their intended audience? Few competing models of the museum offer comparably useful tools.

Nonetheless, as a description, van Mensch's "communication" does not appear to go far enough. By equating the visitor's experience of museum-going with the successful receipt of a message, this notion of the "museum as transmitter" both overestimates the role of the museum's intentions and underestimates the wealth and emotional range of visitor responses. Moreover, its suggestion that museum-going ought be an experience in which, ideally, control lies wholly on the side of the museum seems unacceptable. Also unacceptable (and lacking, as well, in humility) is its implicit suggestion that the museum is a place of one-way communication in which the facts, values, and skills possessed by those responsible for its operation are consistently superior to the facts, values, and skills possessed by its visitors.

Our own common experience of attending museums—an experience that invariably preceded our experience of working in them—ought tell us that this is too restrictive. We all know that museums are *more* than just places of transmission. We know that they are also places of stimulation, not merely of their visitors alone but sometimes of their surrounding communities as well. We know that, sometimes, they can be far more even than that. If we are to have an amended paradigm through which to reorganize the way that we think about museums, then that paradigm must be inclusive enough fully to reflect such a "more." It requires room for the largest vision that those of us who work in museums have of what the museum experience can be.

Such an expanded vision must, moreover, acknowledge that museum visitors may and frequently do have agendas that are not *our* agendas (or, indeed, that the public may have museum-related experiences that are not part of any agenda at all). Museum-goers may legitimately be seeking frivolous diversion, consolation, social status, an opportunity for reverence, companionship, solitude, or innumerable other group or individual goals. Museum-going is neither a tidy nor a predictable activity. Parents and children, visiting a museum for wholly familial reasons, may find themselves unexpectedly awed or even enthralled.

The communication that takes place in a museum may as usefully occur between one visitor and another as between the museum and the visitor.

These experiences ought not be devalued simply because they were not part of our plan. At its finest, least calculable, and most magical moments, the museum can be more than merely a communicator or a stimulant. Museum-going can be a deeply affective experience. In the words with which the AAM's current president Joel N. Bloom closed his 1988 inaugural address, the museum can be and must remain "a place of wonder."

How can we capture this? Might some other term reflect this richness of possibility more adequately than "communicate"? "Make accessible," "make available," and "present" suggest themselves as terms descriptive of what museums do with respect to their collections, but they each appear too passive. Somewhat better might be "provide," i.e., museums not only provide their visiting and nonvisiting publics with access, information, standards, etc., but, as well, provide the setting for important experiences that may be wholly beyond the museum's control or intention. "Provide," though, also seems too passive. The failure thus far to find such a term ought not, however, be thought to undermine this model. Aside from its neatness in constructing a paradigm, the reduction of this broad range of museum experiences to a single term is not really necessary. More important would be to retain its breadth.

Still, if this emerging three-function paradigm appears to be of value, the effort to more fully articulate the range and consequences of its third term ought be pursued. It no longer seems adequate simply to say that this interpretative/exhibition function—essentially a museum's public program—is important because it contributes to (in Robert Hughes's wryly turned phrase) "human betterment." We need to be able to define the purposes for which a museum deals with its public in far finer and more precise ways than we thus far have. Acknowledging how greatly the answers might differ from one museum to another, or even at different times within the history of any single museum, we must be able to say just what a museum would like the outcome of its public program to be. Should this outcome impact a visitor's life in some significant way? If so, in what dimensions, when, how greatly, and how often? Do we believe that this outcome can come about wholly from our own exertions, or do we conceive of the visitor as a collaborator in this effort? Is the impact of the museum limited to its visitors or does its role—as an authority, as an arbiter—extend into the community generally? If so, in what ways, how far, and toward what ends?

Seeking to answer these questions more sharply might help us better to define what it is, ideally, that we envision the museum as doing in its third function. It might also provide us with a more solid justification than we have sometimes heretofore had in seeking the resources that we need to undertake and maintain our other, interconnected and equally vital functions—the preservation and study of our collections. If we can craft a new paradigm even nearly as sturdy as the one that Noble contributed to the museum field in 1970, we will indeed have performed an important service.

MUSEUM MANAGEMENT: WORKERS, COLLECTIONS, AND OTHER CONCERNS

THE WELL-MANAGED
MUSEUM

(EARL F. CHEIT, COAUTHOR)

Summarizing his twenty-nine-year tenure (1908–37) as director of Cambridge University's Fitzwilliam Museum, the late S. C. Cockerell said, "I found it a pig sty; I turned it into a palace." If we assume that Cockerell meant to describe something more than just positive changes in the Fitzwilliam's physical facilities—that he referred as well to improvements in its collections, staff, finances, governance, records, and public image—then his remark might serve as a neat shorthand summary of good management. Good management is to move an organization from the "here" of a less well managed condition to the "there" of a better managed one— from being something near a pig sty toward being something like a palace. The aim of good management is to have a well-managed museum.

What do we mean by a well-managed museum? The clearest indications that a museum is well managed might be its ability to demonstrate that it makes the most efficient and effective use possible of the resources which it has available. In day-to-day practice, however, it is only rarely that a museum can be measured on so all-encompassing a scale. Most frequently, the degree to which a museum is well managed—or could, at least, be better managed—can only be determined by examining a number of more detailed and specific factors that relate to its programs, planning capability, governance, staff, finances, facilities, collections, records, and outside relationships.

What, then, might some of these factors be? What are some of the attributes of a well-managed museum? The following nonprioritized list (on which a number of entries may overlap) is intended to be suggestive rather than exhaustive:

- a clearly defined mission and set of shared long-term goals and underlying values;

- the ability to formulate and to pursue such strategies as may be necessary to acquire, process, and expend the resources that it needs to fulfill its mission together with an array of ongoing and successive programs that readily relate to—and demonstrably further—that mission;

- the ability to formulate and to adhere to long-term and short-term budgets, timetables, and other operational plans consistent with its various strategies;

- a structure of governance that provides for wise oversight, a long-range institutional view, and access to the varied resources that may be necessary to produce its programs;

- a commitment to develop the managerial and vocational skills and knowledge of its staff;

- a competent, loyal, stable, mutually respectful, well-motivated and well-led staff that is able to work with relative independence in pursuit of a series of agreed-upon and well-understood goals;

- appropriate physical facilities that are maintained in good repair and provide adequate space for the production of its various programs;

- a system for implementing each of its functions such as, for example:

  - closely followed policies for the acquisition and management of its collections that assure their proper physical care; that provide for the maintenance of appropriate records as to their identification, location, condition, and provenance; and that assure their maximum public accessibility consistent with their care;

  - information management systems that permit the swift, accurate retrieval of the data necessary to manage its resources and to produce its various programs;

  - financial systems that operate to keep the expenditures of resources within budgeted targets, that keep management accurately advised as to the museum's current status, and that serve as the basis for providing timely reports to various outside individuals and authorities;

- a capacity to resolve issues related to the diversity of its present and potential staff and markets by continually renewing and, where necessary, modifying its practices and programs;

- a sensitivity to the needs and wishes of its existing and potential patrons and markets sufficiently acute that it can make considered decisions about the extent, if any, to which its programs will be shaped to meet those needs and wishes;

- the maintenance of a positive public image through which the actions of the institution and its staff are consistently and broadly perceived as related to the pursuit of the institution's mission and goals rather than any undisclosed or self-serving agenda; and

• the maintenance of a favorable legal status pursuant to which the institution will continue to be exempt from federal, state, and local income taxes, donors will continue to be able to claim charitable deductions for their contributions, and the museum will continue to enjoy whatever other privileges may be extended by its locality to not-for-profit organizations.

No claim is made that the presence of any or most or even all of these attributes would in itself be sufficient to make a museum an excellent institution. Management, even at its best, is only a single dimension of a museum's overall operation. Excellence in a museum must depend as well on the quality of its educational and other programs, the importance of its purpose and the disciplinary value of its collection. Nonetheless, it is difficult to conceive that a poorly managed museum would ever be able to achieve and to sustain a level of excellence for any extended time. Good management may not be the measure of a good museum but, in the long run, it would most certainly appear to be one of its critical prerequisites.

IN PURSUIT OF A PROFESSION

The Status of Museum Work in America

E arly in the nineteenth century—first in Great Britain and then spreading to the United States—a new phenomenon appeared in the workplace. Sociologists now call it "professionalization." It was a process by which a group of workers who were engaged in a common occupation could, through their own effort, achieve public recognition that their work constituted a distinct "profession" and that each of them—as a practitioner of that profession—was entitled to the special respect that is due a "professional." Whereas only physicians, lawyers, and the clergy—the practitioners of the so-called learned professions of medicine, law and theology—had been accorded such status in the early 1800s, by the early 1900s we find that architects, nurses, librarians, dentists, accountants, pharmacists, engineers, social workers, and opticians—among others—had all succeeded in achieving professional recognition in either Britain or the United States, or both.

Originally prepared as the keynote address for the 1987 annual meeting of the Council of Australian Museum Associations, Brisbane, Queensland, September 1987. Reprinted, with permission, from *Museum News,* November/December 1988. Copyright © 1988, American Association of Museums. All rights reserved.

I

In the years since, this process has continued at an accelerated pace. Occupational groups that span the gamut from airline pilots to zookeepers have engaged in what one sociologist has described as "heroic struggles for professional identification."[1] For the members of these groups, the reward has often justified the struggle. In an open society, professionalism has the power to confer upon its practitioners some of that same elevated prestige that might elsewhere be obtained only by the accumulation of wealth or through aristocratic birth. What it has offered—and continues to offer—is what Magali Sarfatti Larson has called the "novel possibility of gaining status through work."[2]

Among those who have struggled for professional identification in the United States are American museum workers. The professionalism they have sought is not just the simple professionalism of those who—like professional golfers, musicians, or masseurs—are paid for their work as distinct from amateurs or volunteers who are not. It has been the richer, far more complex professionalism of belonging to what is recognized by the public to be a "profession."

Some believe that American museum workers have already succeeded in achieving this status. Others doubt that they ever can. Most, including myself, think that significant progress has been made but that much remains to be done. I think that almost everybody, however, would agree that many important improvements in American museums themselves have come about as a by-product of this struggle by museum workers to gain professional identification.

II

In Webster's *Third New International Dictionary*, a "profession" is defined as:

A calling requiring specialized knowledge and often long and intensive preparation including instruction in skills and methods as well as in the scientific, historical, or scholarly principles underlying such skills and methods, maintaining by force of organization or concerted opinion high standards of achievement and conduct, and committing its members to continued study and to a kind of work which has for its prime purpose the rendering of a public service.

To this dictionary definition, most sociologists would add the attribute of autonomy and the observation that, in the most highly evolved professions such as medicine and law, the practitioners of the profession may themselves actually prescribe and monitor the preparatory training for the field, control the entry of new practitioners, and not only promulgate standards of achievement and conduct but also enforce these standards by imposing sanctions upon those who violate them.

In the official literature of the American museum field, it has long been taken for granted that museum work is *already* well recognized as a single and distinct "profession" and that, accordingly, those who work in museums are, *ipso facto,* "professionals." The *Code of Ethics* adopted in 1985 by the Council of Australian Museum Associations appears to make a similar assumption. The International Council of Museums (ICOM) similarly assumes that the existence of a "museum profession" is a given. In Article 5 of the ICOM *Statutes* it defines this profession to consist of: "all the personnel of museums . . . having received a specialized technical or academic training or possessing an equivalent practical experience, and respecting a fundamental code of professional ethics."

Those who doubt that museum work can ever be recognized as a distinct profession focus chiefly on the problem of diversity—the diversity of disciplines *among* museums and the diversity of the knowledge and skills required *within* any particular museum. In a closely reasoned paper delivered at the annual meeting of the American Association of Museums (AAM) in Detroit in 1985, my Smithsonian colleague Wilcomb E. Washburn questioned whether there really was *any* unique body of knowledge or set of skills that could be found in museums of every discipline and which could provide the unifying basis for a single profession.³ In essence, he asked how a botanist in a natural history museum could be linked to the exhibits designer in a history museum, or how either of them could be linked to the development officer of an art museum, as members of the same profession.

A similar position was taken in a frequently cited paper published some two decades ago by Albert E. Parr—then the senior scientist at the American Museum of Natural History.⁴ The people working in museums, he said, were largely professionals but not members of the same profession. They belonged to a variety of different professions. What could, he suggested, provide museum people with a "mutually beneficial solidarity" was not to imagine a commonality either of their daily tasks or of their qualification to perform these tasks but to focus instead on the commonality of the goals which they sought to attain.

Whether these critics are correct that the inherent diversity of museum work is such that it can never be classified as a single profession may not, however, be wholly relevant. More to the point, I think, is our understanding of how beneficial an impact this pursuit of professionalism has had and can continue to have on our museums themselves. As William the Silent observed, "It is not necessary . . . to succeed in order to persevere." And, as one American museum worker has pointed out, professionalism should not properly be thought of as an end in itself but, rather, as a "ritual behavior through which we seek to accomplish larger purposes."⁵ In the end, it must of course be those "larger purposes," and not the enhancement of our own individual status, that museum work is about. With that as a background, let us now see what has thus far been accomplished in this pursuit.

III

In acquiring the various attitudes, structures and practices that distinguish a professionalized occupation from mere employment, museum workers in the United States have been eminently successful with respect to at least four: first, in having developed the attitude that they follow a calling which has for its prime purpose the rendering of a public service; second, in their establishment and maintenance of a variety of strong—albeit, not necessarily well-coordinated—national, regional, and local organizations to deal directly with professional concerns; third, in having created an institutional accreditation program that emphasizes high standards of achievement; and fourth, in having promulgated standards of ethical conduct applicable both to the museum field as a whole and to the various specialties within it.

Particularly striking is the degree to which museum work has come to be regarded as altruistic—the sense that museum employees are not working merely for wages but are following a calling intended to benefit other individuals and the community at large. To say this is not to say that American museum workers do not expect to be fairly compensated for their work—they may even, as has been the case in several American museums, form unions and go on strike to enforce that expectation—but it is to say that compensation does not appear to be the driving force behind their choice of occupation. Whereas there may well be other occupations—banking, advertising, and insurance, for example—in which employees who positively dislike what they do nonetheless "can't quit" because they need the salary or security that their jobs provide, American museum work, in general, neither pays enough nor offers enough tenured positions to keep many people in it who would rather be doing something else. In fact, one of the things that makes museum association meetings so exciting—it may even be why we have so many of them—is the opportunity they offer to be together with other people who are so genuinely interested in and enthusiastic about what they do. American musems are, for the most part, remarkably pleasant places in which to work.

Also striking has been the proliferation and growth of the various organizations in which museum workers have associated themselves to strive together for common goals. Beginning with the establishment of the American Association of Museums in 1906, there are today more than eighty different state, regional, disciplinary, or occupationally specialized associations, councils, societies, and committees to which museums and/or museum workers may belong. The AAM alone counts some ten thousand members—two thousand institutions and eight thousand individuals. That these organizations provide American museum workers with an important means by which to exchange information and establish valuable collegial networks seems too evident to require elaboration.

Among the more evolved professions, however, such professional associations are generally expected to fulfill a number of other roles as well: to prescribe and monitor the academic training required for entry into the field, to provide programs of continuing education, to publish scholarly research, to promulgate and enforce standards of achievement and conduct, and to represent and defend the political interests of their constituent members.

In the United States, at least, the record of museum associations in fulfilling these other roles has been decidedly mixed. Where they have been most successful is in their political role—they have served as skilled and vigorous legislative advocates for museums—and in their promulgation of standards of achievement and conduct. Where they have been less successful—a point to which I will return—is in devising ways to enforce these standards, especially standards of conduct. With respect to continuing education, they have done relatively well—particularly at the regional level. With regard to research and scholarly publications, their record is not as good. Where they have failed almost entirely, however—another point to which I will return—is in relation to the academic training that is currently offered for entry into the field.

Notwithstanding any such shortcomings, however, these American museum organizations—and the AAM in particular—have provided American museum workers with perhaps the most persuasive of their arguments that they have now achieved—or, at least, are very close to—full professional status. This has been through the AAM's success in promulgating standards of achievement and conduct.

The standards of achievement are to be found in the program of institutional accreditation that the AAM initiated in 1970. By combining a rigorous process of self-examination with peer reviews conducted by on-site visiting committees, the accreditation program seeks to assure that museums adhere to "attainable professional standards of quality and performance."[6] Virtually all of those most familiar with this program agree that these "attainable professional standards" have been steadily rising during the seventeen years since the program's inception. There are, incidentally, some 650 museums currently accredited. While this number is less than a third of the AAM's total institutional membership, it does include almost every large museum in the country. For smaller institutions, which have tended to shy away from accreditation, a companion program—the Museum Assessment Program (MAP)—has proven a valuable adjunct in this effort to raise standards.

The AAM has also been active in promulgating standards of conduct. These have taken the form of codes of ethics. The first of these was a *Code of Ethics for Museum Workers* that the AAM adopted in 1925.[7] Interestingly, the words "profession" or "professional" appear nowhere in it. Of the various codes promulgated in the years since, the most widely known is *Museum Ethics* (1978). As evidence that the way museum workers think about themselves had changed during the fifty years between these two AAM codes, consider that—in the latter—references to the "profession" and "professionalism" abound. To date, nearly thirty thousand copies of this code have been printed and distributed. A committee of the AAM is currently at work revising this 1978 code to bring it into greater conformity with the code of professional ethics ICOM adopted in 1986.

IV

If those, then, are some of the things that we who work in American museums have accomplished in our pursuit of professionalism, where have we failed and how might these failures be remedied? Our four most evident failures, it seems to me, relate to the question of individual autonomy, to the supervision of preparatory training, to the entry of new practitioners into the field, and to the enforcement of ethical standards.

Autonomy has traditionally been considered one of the attributes of a professional. Our very sense of a professional is that such a person relies primarily on his or her own expertise and seasoned judgment in coming to a decision. Here, though, we encounter a difficulty. Even if we concede that there already *is* a museum profession, it is not one which—like medicine or law—can be practiced alone. Museum work can only be performed in an organizational setting. Can a curator, who must necessarily work under the immediate authority of a director and/or other senior staff as well as the remote authority of a lay board of trustees or other governing structure, truly be autonomous?

The AAM's 1978 ethics code sought to answer this in the affirmative. It provided: "Responsibility for the final decisions will normally rest with the museum administration and all employees are expected to support these decisions; but no staff member can be required to reverse, alter or suppress his professional judgment in order to conform to a management decision."[8] What this fails to acknowledge is the swiftness with which a nontenured employee who consistently fails to conform to management decisions may become a former employee. This tension between professional autonomy and organizational structure is not unique to museums. The problem of the salaried professional is a pervasive twentieth-century phenomenon. The physician employed in a drug-testing program for a pharmaceutical company cannot expect to exercise the same authority and responsibility as does a doctor in private practice. The chemist who works for a pesticide manufacturer will rarely enjoy the creative independence of his university-based fellow professional. And the curator who works in a museum simply cannot be given any formal grant of autonomy that would transcend the museum's organizational needs.

The American sociologist Harold Wilensky has suggested that this lack of formal autonomy may be to some degree offset if the employing organization is itself "infused with professional-ism."9 In our own case, it might also be offset by the fact that museums—as nonprofit organizations—are organized around a mission of service, not profit, and accordingly have goals that should parallel the altruistic motives of those who work in them. Thus, Wilensky's own conclusion on this point would seem to be applicable to museums, i.e., that, in appropriate circumstances and in actual practice "the salaried professional may have more autonomy in his work than those self-employed professionals whose relatively low income forces them to scramble for many clients or who depend on the patronage of a few powerful [ones]."10

That those who work in American museums have not taken a more responsible role in the preparation of students for museum work continues to be a major defect in their claim that their work constitutes a distinct profession. The problem here is two-fold. It involves first, the enormous and unsupervised proliferation in recent years of so-called "museum studies" programs. More fundamental, though, is the question of whether these programs are truly the best preparation for working in a museum.

A recent survey by the Smithsonian Institution's Office of Museum Programs found no fewer than 325 museum training opportunities offered in the United States alone. These range in magnitude from graduate level university-based programs to workshops and symposia. No less than eighteen are degree-granting programs in which museological courses constitute 50 percent or more of the required study. As yet there is no formal system in place by which to accredit these programs, or even to evaluate them. Some, such as the graduate program in museum studies at George Washington University or the program offered by the Center for Museum Studies at John F. Kennedy University in San Francisco, are under able leadership, provide students with the opportunity to study with well-respected museum practitioners, and offer the chance to obtain practical experience through internships in soundly managed museums or allied organizations. At the other end of the spectrum are nondegree programs that appear to have been developed solely to meet a market demand from students and that have little or no access to the actual day-to-day working practices of museums.

Thus far, the AAM has not felt itself able to penetrate very deeply into this thicket. During the 1970s, it did publish a curriculum guide for these programs and, more recently, a set of criteria by which such programs ought be evaluated.[11] Subsequently, a self-study guide and accompanying questionnaire were developed by the AAM's Museum Studies Committee between 1983 and 1985, but have never been published or widely distributed. Beyond these efforts, however, the organized museum field has taken no steps to assure either that those who hold themselves out to teach so-called museum studies are actually competent to do so or that those who have mastered these studies are actually prepared to work in a museum.

When we turn to the question of whether such programs really are the best—or even an adequate—preparation for working in a museum, the fact that strikes one immediately is that many—perhaps even a majority—of those who hold responsible positions in American museums have never had any specific academic training in museology. They are largely cultural historians or botanists or art historians who learned about museum work by working in museums.

The heart of the dictionary definition of a profession is that it requires a "specialized knowledge" that its practitioners hold in common. Here we must return to the diversity problem raised earlier by Washburn and Parr. Once we separate out the discipline-based knowledge of history, science, or art held by our directors, curators, and educators and the theory-based technical expertise of our conservators, registrars, and graphic designers, what remains left to be called museology? Something, certainly—some of it to do with such practical matters as tidiness (keeping track of things, and keeping them in good repair) and much of it to do with community service—but is this body of knowledge extensive enough or sufficiently profound to require its own course of study? Might not this remaining museological balance be readily bundled into a compact one or two semester course entitled "Introduction to Museum Methods and Practices" and offered as an adjunct to graduate-level discipline studies?

Is it possible that, in the intensity of our desire to be considered a profession, we have simply assumed the existence of a body of theoretical knowledge that is not really there?[12] The question is an important one. While our aspirations toward professionalism may be at stake, at even greater critical risk are the thousands of dollars and years of time that students eager to work in museums might far better spend in discipline-based programs instead of in "museum studies." If any broader training, most particularly training in management were subsequently to be needed, then mid-career programs might be the best vehicle for that.

Should those who work in museums control the entry of new practitioners into the field? The imposition of such controls has certainly been the pattern among the more highly evolved professions where licensing or certification procedures are the common practice. For museums, though, I think we would make a terrible mistake if, in our zeal to be thought about as professionals, we should ever go that far. In the museums of the United States, at least, those who work in museums come from a remarkable variety of backgrounds, have found their way to museums by an equally remarkable variety of paths, and are called upon to perform a still equally remarkable variety of tasks. It is perhaps this very fact that seems to give our museums so much of their individuality and vitality. In fact, there currently seems to be little or no sympathy in the United States for controlling the entry into museum work. If that constitutes a failure in our pursuit of professionalism, then it's a failure we should be prepared to accept.

The final question, then, and perhaps the most important of all, is whether those of us who work in museums can ever attain that degree of professionalism in which we might play a major role not merely in prescribing standards of achievement and conduct for our field but in enforcing these as well. This, after all, has been the ultimate goal of every professional project—to transfer the control of the work one does away from those who may not fully understand or appreciate it and give it, instead, to a group of one's colleagues who share a common training, practical experience, and set of sympathetic values.

Let me pause here for a brief anecdote. In 1984, newspapers throughout the United States published a series of horrendous revelations about certain unsavory practices that had been discovered at the Atlanta, Georgia, municipal zoo. When reporters reached the American Association of Zoological Parks and Aquariums (AAZPA), the umbrella professional organization that very much parallels our AAM, to ask what the AAZPA planned to do about the situation, the AAZPA was able to respond, first, that it had already been aware of the problem and, second, that it had suspended the Atlanta Zoo from association membership many months earlier.

Without doubt, the single and widely reported fact that there was a professional organization in place which was capable of policing its field and able to take disciplinary action against an offending member forestalled what might likely have been an investigation of zoos throughout the United States. The Atlanta problem was confined to Atlanta. That the AAZPA was able to act as it did was because it has, in recent years, increasingly tied membership to accreditation to the point where, since the end of 1985, accreditation has actually become mandatory for any zoo or aquarium seeking to continue its membership.

Would a similar result have followed if the offending institution had been an American museum instead of a zoo? The answer, alas, must be: emphatically not. If the museum had been accredited, then the suspension of its accreditation might have been one possibility. Even in that, though, great care would have been needed. In the most highly publicized instance in which the AAM suspended a museum's accreditation—that of the Vanderilt Museum in Long Island, New York, whose accreditation was suspended in 1980 for perceived inadequacies in the care of its collection—the museum was able to take the AAM into court and to question the fairness of the procedures it had followed.[13]

Whether a hypothetically offending museum could also be disciplined by suspending it from AAM membership is by no means clear. The AAM's constitution and bylaws provide only the limited right to withdraw membership from those individuals or institutions who use their membership "to work for purposes inconsistent with the aims" of the AAM or have not paid their dues.[14] For any lesser disciplinary sanctions such as reprimand or censure, there are no provisions at all. And, unlike the 1985 *Code of Ethics,* which permits the Council of Australian Museum Associations to recommend disciplinary actions for serious breaches by individuals at least, no comparable provision appears anywhere in the AAM's 1978 code of ethics.[15]

In the United States, the exercise of formal police power by an association group is beyond question a matter of considerable legal complexity. Equally clear is that there are many informal means by which the museum field enforces its standards over both the individuals and institutions within it. A high degree of "colleague consciousness" is another of the attributes often ascribed to professionals, and for museum workers who aspire to such a status the impact of peer pressure can be an important deterrent against breaching standards of achievement or conduct. Nonetheless, it seems to me unthinkable that we can ever advance the pursuit of professionalism very much further in American museums unless and until we begin to deal squarely with this issue of enforcement.

V

In the end, of course, whether the claim of American museum workers to be professionals will be honored by anyone but themselves must depend not upon their own image of themselves but upon the public's. Is the work they do perceived to be unique? Are they considered competent to be entrusted with the execution of tasks that the public thinks important? Addressing these questions nearly a generation ago, G. Ellis Burcaw unhappily observed:

> The image of the museum in America is that anyone who has nothing better to do can manage the community museum, and that (except for the jobs that obviously require special skills and knowledge, such as taxidermy or the restoration of paintings) practically anyone can be used to staff practically any museum.[16]

Is this observation still valid? To some degree, I suspect that it is. In part, of course, that may be an ironic byproduct of the skill with which we do our jobs. In a well-run museum, the staff should be largely invisible. Quite properly, it is to the objects that we have given the pride of place.

Beyond that, however, Burcaw's observation may suggest that we ought exercise some restraint in the claims that we make to the public. While we understand that the delicacy and skill required to care for or conserve a fragile object may sometimes be comparable to that required to perform open heart surgery, the public does not necessarily acknowledge these to be equally matters of life and death, and neither should we. While we understand that an object once lost may be lost forever, the public understands that an object is not a life. As Brian Morris of the United Kingdom Museums and Galleries Commission reminded attendees of the 1983 ICOM triennial in London, "All the objects in your museum, be they never so rare, never so precious, are not more important than one single human life among those who come to see your treasure."[17]

The great prestige that was accorded to those who practiced the learned professions—medicine, law, and theology—was not grounded merely on the fact that they were "professionals." It was based upon the awesome magnitude of the matters with which they regularly dealt: life, death, liberty, and salvation. We deal with lesser things. While some greater public recognition of our efforts would certainly be gratifying, it might nonetheless be wise for us to keep our claims proportionate.

Our gratification aside, however, would a greater public understanding of the distinctive nature of museum work have some other importance? I think it would. Such an understanding could, in turn, lead to a more sensitive public recognition of the distinctive nature of museums themselves. In the United States, the most common public view of museums is that they are either dusty depositories for things that are dead or places of recreation that might provide for an afternoon's lively entertainment. Rare has been any broad public understanding that museums might also be—that they might even primarily be—socially relevant institutions with the skills to collect, preserve, and exhibit objects in ways that not only deepen our understanding of the past but also enrich our lives and enhance in powerful ways our ability to shape a better future for ourselves, our descendants, and our communities. These may not be immediate matters of life or death, but neither are they not important.

Here, then—at least in the American experience—is where our pursuit of professionalism might legitimately end: with the realization that our quest for professional recognition may or may not ever be successful but that the byproducts of this effort are both positive and extremely important. First, to the extent that, in our pursuit of professional status, we apply ever-increasing standards of achievement and conduct to the work we do, then—at the same time—we are helping to move the museums that we serve toward their fullest potential. And second, in seeking to draw the public's attention to the value of this work we do, we also stimulate a broader understanding of how significant a role these museums might play in making better, richer lives for all of us, both as individuals and as members of a community. If we are able to do these things, then whether or not we ever achieve the status of "professionals" might, to my thinking, be besides the point. We will still have served a larger purpose.

Notes

1. Harold Wilensky, "The Professionalization of Everyone?" *The American Journal of Sociology,* September (1964): 137.

2. *The Rise of Professionalism: A Sociological Analysis* (Berkeley, California: University of California Press, 1977): 5.

3. Subsequently published in *Museum News,* December 1985, as "Professionalizing the Museum."

4. "A Plurality of Professions," *Curator,* 7 (4), 1964.

5. Scott Swank, "Peer Review: What's in it for You?" *Museum News* (December 1985): 32.

6. *Professional Standards for Museum Accreditation* (Washington, D.C.: American Association of Museums, 1978): 8.

7. Reproduced in Marilyn Phelan, *Museums and the Law* (Nashville, Tenn.: American Association for State and Local History, 1982): 252–57.

8. *Museum Ethics* (Washington, D.C.: American Association of Museums, 1978): 23.

9. Wilensky, note 1 *supra,* at 147.

10. *Idem.*

11. For a summary of these activities, see "Criteria for Examining Professional Museum Studies Programs," *Museum News* (June 1983): 70.

12. For a pertinent discussion, see the paper by Geoffrey D. Lewis in *Museological Working Papers No. 1* (Stockholm, Sweden, ICOM Committee for Museology, 1980), at 27.

13. For a fuller account, see Stephen E. Weil, "Breaches of Trust, Remedies, and Standards in the American Private Art Museum," in *Beauty and the Beasts* (Washington, D.C.: Smithsonian Institution Press, 1983), at 178, 185–86.

14. American Association of Museums Constitution Article III, Section 7; Bylaws Chapter I, Section 3.

15. Section II, 18.2, *Code of Ethics for Art, History and Science Museums* (Kingston, Australia: Council of Australian Museum Associations, 1985): 29.

16. "Museum Training: The Responsibility of College and University Museums," *Museum News* (April 1969): 15.

17. Proceedings, 15.

COLEMAN'S VISION OF
THE MUSEUM WORKER:
IS IT STILL VALID TODAY?

P*lus ça change, plus c'est la même chose.*
The more things change, the more they remain the same. Fifty years have passed since Laurence Vail Coleman examined the situation of the American museum worker. In the interim, the United States has fought three wars and seen nine new presidents take office. Computers have changed the way we keep our records. Facsimile machines have changed the way we communicate. The 7,500 museum workers that Coleman was able to identify in 1939 have meanwhile swollen to a number at least ten times that size. Such changes notwithstanding, Coleman's prescience has proven remarkable. As applicable today as when he first set them down are his descriptions of the diverse callings that these museum workers follow, of the various ways in which they are (and are not) rewarded for their efforts and—perhaps most importantly—of their potential to form themselves into a distinct profession.

Of perhaps the greatest relevance today is Coleman's sharp insight that museum work could not further approach professional status until its followers were collectively prepared both to "set standards of attainment" and to "take up group respon-

This article originally appeared in *The Museologist* magazine, Vol. 52, No. 180, and is reprinted courtesy of the Mid-Atlantic Association of Museums.

sibility." Some thirty more years were needed to attain the first of these goals. It was only after the publication of the *Belmont Report* in 1968 that the American Association of Museums initiated its accreditation program in 1970. The second of these goals, however—the assumption by museum workers of some form of "group responsibility"—continues to be elusive. Fifty years later, those who work in museums are only now and for the first time beginning seriously to explore how their various pronouncements with respect to ethics can be coupled with some practical mode of enforcement. "Better late than never," the ever-patient Coleman might likely have said, and enthusiastically applauded the effort.

Less clear, however, is whether Coleman also recognized that this exploration might in time produce a considerable tension—if not an outright contradiction—between two of his principal desiderata. On the one hand, he clearly hoped to see museum work further professionalized through the assumption of "group responsibility." On the other, he believed in the appointment and retention of strong museum directors—charismatic leaders whose spirits might come to permeate their institutions and to animate their staffs. For those below the directorial level, this tension could ultimately translate into a dilemma of divided loyalties, a situation in which they might find themselves torn between two conflicting forces—one that pulled at them horizontally, the other vertically.

Under such a scenario, the horizontal pull would be exercised by their colleagues—within the museum, across the country, and even possibly worldwide—with their assertion of a series of professional "oughts" that were derived from the evolving standards and values of the museum field as a whole. Intersecting with these—sometimes, in fact, cutting sharply against them— would be those downwardly felt and hierarchically enforced "musts" that are minimally required for the orderly operation of any particular institution. So long as these forces remained in harmony, museum workers might face little problem. But what would be expected of them when no such harmony prevailed?

When these obligations came into conflict, how was such a conflict to be resolved?

Such a conflict does not yield to so simple an analysis as does the more familiar one of conflict of interest. To deal with the latter, there is a recent and copious body of literature which agrees, in general, on a principal point. In any conflict between a worker's own interest and that of the museum, the museum's interest is to be paramount. Under the professionalism scenario, however—where the conflict to be dealt with is wholly external to the worker and the competing interests may all be deemed legitimate—no such literature has yet evolved to serve the museum worker as a guide.

How might Coleman himself have approached such a conflict? My own reading of him suggests that, pushed to the extreme of an either/or, he would have inclined (sadly, perhaps, but nonetheless firmly) against the horizontal pull of peer pressure and toward the orderly management of the individual institution. While Coleman recognized the possibility that museum work might be professionalized—and certainly placed a high value on the attributes that such work might acquire in the quest of that status—he also had an extremely practical view of what was required in order for a museum organization to be effective. Needed, above all, was a centrality of purpose.

Describing the late 1930s practices of some larger American museums in which the basic program planning had been almost entirely delegated to the curatorial staff, Coleman was sharply critical. Such a practice, he wrote, "overlooks the need for unity of an institution under coherent leadership. A museum should be able to throw its whole organized strength into the accomplishment of its aims—but this is not possible if it is an arena where independent forces act freely, often at cross purposes."

Similarly, in discussing the problem of overly specialized curators—at one point he likened such curators to a kind of spider that builds a cunningly concealed nest where it can pursue its own interests free of outside observation—he suggested that this problem could not be solved "until trustees and directors conceive of the museum as an integrated whole rather than as a group of airtight compartments."

While much else that Coleman wrote about museum work remains apt today—extraordinary is the clarity with which he saw that museum interpretive programs could only suffer when they were relegated to an education department separate from (and almost invariably subordinate to) the curatorial departments—his principal teaching may still be this: that the museum can only realize its fullest potential when those within it are united in their effort by some shared and single vision.

To conclude thus is not to suggest that the positive attributes of professionalism are irrelevant to the pursuit of such a vision. Indeed, the standards and values that the quest for professionalism may generate—no less the sense of altruism that such a quest may engender—can prove critically important in achieving whatever excellence a museum does finally attain. Nonetheless, the claims of professionalism must be tempered. In the end, it is not the field as a whole but only the museum—as a particular institution under specific leadership—that is capable of such an attainment. In the long run also (or so Coleman would seem to suggest), it is to *that* institution, and not to his or her far-flung colleagues, that the museum worker's primary loyalty must finally be directed.

The West Coast legal ethicist Michael Josephson has distinguished between what he calls "dog loyalty" or loyalty to the master, and "cat loyalty" or loyalty to the house. Many observers, Josephson included, would opt for "cat loyalty" as the sounder course. Coleman, with his penchant for strong leadership—"The director is the museum," he once wrote—might not have wholly agreed. Certainly, however, he would have considered either to be an attribute far superior to "wolf loyalty" or loyalty to the pack. Fifty years later, that still would seem to be the right choice.

THE MORE EFFECTIVE DIRECTOR: SPECIALIST OR GENERALIST?

Discipline specialist or management generalist? The immediate question posed is which of them might be more effective as the director of a museum, a horticultural garden, or a similar interpretive/preservative organization—an individual solidly grounded in the organization's particular discipline (or at least a kindred discipline) or somebody whose training has been in management generally and whose experience has been in some other field.

Rather than attempt to answer this directly, I will digress to consider three other questions. The answers to those should, in turn, help us to address the original query. Throughout this digression, the word "museum" should be understood to include the entire range of interpretive/preservative organizations (including horticultural gardens), and "he" and "his" are, of course, intended also to include "she" and "hers."

The three other questions are:

Can museum presentations be value neutral, or do they inescapably reflect a point of view?

If such presentations do inescapably reflect a point of view, is it necessary or desirable that this point of view be consistent throughout a museum?

If it is necessary or desirable that a consistent point of view be reflected throughout a museum, then whose point of view should it be?

Can museum presentations be value neutral? Rene d'Harnoncourt—the late director of New York City's Museum of Modern Art—is supposed to have said, "Simply to place an object is to interpret it." This seems correct. To select a particular object for exhibit, to put that object into juxtaposition with other objects and to dispose of those juxtapositions in a three-dimensional gallery space—these are all interpretative acts. As such, they must necessarily to a degree be colored by our values, our beliefs, our interests, and our taste. Each of us has a truth, but all of our truths are not the same.

Journalists try to distinguish between what is reportage and what is editorial (albeit that there are some who doubt that any such distinction is even possible). Museum presentations, however, are almost invariably editorial. They do more than simply report. For the most part, they also argue, they urge, they seek to convince. What makes a great museum exhibition memorable to us is not its dispassionate quality or the objective skill with which it describes or documents some particular phenomenon. To the contrary, what makes such an exhibition memorable is its capacity to move us, to provide us with a fresh outlook, to induce in us a sense of revelation. Describing the new Holocaust Museum soon to be built in Washington, its director has said the effect it will strive for is "emotive."

Even if objectivity were to be our goal, the very physicality of the museum enterprise might well limit our ability to achieve it. The *New York Times* may have enough space to carry "All the News that's Fit to Print." Those who deal in objects have no comparable luxury. They must of necessity be selective. This at once means that judgment and connoisseurship—neither of them value neutral—must come into play. Invariably, these will be functions of our values, beliefs, interests, and taste. Inescapably, they will reflect some point of view.

Is it necessary or desirable that this point of view be consistent throughout a museum? Those who argue against such consistency generally do so from one of two assumptions—either, first, that the museum has a basic obligation to be "fair" and to present all legitimate points of view or else, second, that the members of the museum's curatorial staff enjoy some equivalent of academic freedom that thereby entitles them to present a variety of differing views.

A dramatic effort to establish the "fairness" argument occurred in the late 1970s when several creationist groups brought a lawsuit against the Smithsonian Institution's National Museum of Natural History. Their claim was that the museum was—through its exhibits—both implicitly and explicitly endorsing a Darwinian theory of evolution. Among the remedies they asked was that the court direct the museum to give equal exposure to their own creationist point of view.

While this lawsuit was dismissed for reasons not germane here, the "equal treatment" question it raised must be considered. Are museums required to be "fair?" Should museums be treated like radio and television stations, which must, by law, give "equal time" to rival political candidates and observe a "fairness doctrine" with respect to controversial public issues? Or should museums be treated like newspapers and periodicals, which are constitutionally protected against any such public interference and retain the unbridled right to espouse their own views and to exclude the views of those with whom they disagree?

In a free society, it is the restraint imposed on broadcasters—and not the privilege extended to a free press—that is the anomaly. "Equal time" and the "fairness doctrine" were not established as being in themselves desiderata. They were simply the byproducts of a licensing system mandated by the scarcity of available broadcasting frequencies and the perceived public need to allot these on some orderly basis. Our broadcasting laws were intended to assure that the monopoly granted to operate a particular frequency did not permit the operator also to monopolize the points of view that could be broadcast over that frequency.

There is no parallel here for museums. While the resources available to museums may sometimes seem scarce, the fact remains that the public is entitled to have all of the museums—and all of the points of view—that it wants and is prepared to support. To require that museums be licensed would be no more tolerable in a free society than to require licenses of newspapers or magazines. In the same vein, to require that a museum fairly represent every point of view would be as intolerable as prohibiting a newspaper from endorsing a political candidate or a magazine from taking an editorial position on a controversial issue. If creationists do not like what they find in an existing natural history museum, then the proper solution is for them to start a museum of their own in which they will be free to adopt and disseminate whatever point of view they want. The fairness argument has no application to such an open-ended situation.

What, then, of the argument that members of the curatorial staff have, or should have, some equivalent of academic freedom? Are not museums, as educational institutions, somewhat akin to colleges and universities? If so, does not a curator occupy a position that parallels that of a faculty member? If so, may he not then be entitled to employ the museum's programs and facilities as vehicles through which to express his own personal convictions and preferences on matters that fall within the scope of the museum's subject matter?

The difficulty with this argument is its assumption that academic freedom has evolved primarily as a right or benefit conferred upon those by whom it might be exercised. What this argument fails to recognize is that the evolution of academic freedom must be seen as inseparable from the development of the medieval university in which faculty and students conjoined to form an academic community. Neither the history nor structure of the museum parallels that of the university. The differences between them might well be symbolized by the titles generally conferred upon their highest executive officers. The museum has a director who directs. The college has a president who presides.

Beyond this, moreover, the relationship of museum curators to museum visitors is in no sense anything like the relationship between faculty members and students. In contrast to the faculty member's obligation to his students, the curator's basic responsibilities are to the administration by which he has been hired and to the collections entrusted to his care. While that administration may invite his participation in formulating an institutional viewpoint—he might for example serve on a curatorial committee that reviews the museum's programs—the argument that he is independently entitled to use the museum's facilities to present his own point of view in opposition to the administration's does not seem to carry weight. Curators are not tenured, and notwithstanding that their scholarly concerns may be similar to those of university faculty members, they are not teachers and do not function as part of an academic community.

What about the other side? If these arguments *against* consistency fail, is the argument *for* consistency any better? I would argue that it is. Museums must rely on continuing support from outside patrons. Those most likely to be supportive are those who share an institution's values. Unless such values are projected in some consistent and coherent way, such support may be difficult to obtain.

Imagine, for example, the situation of a natural history museum in which the departments of entomology and botany both took an actively positive view toward a Darwinian theory of evolution while the department of invertebrate zoology opposed such a theory with equal vigor. Or imagine an art museum in which the curator of prints was collecting the work of Leroy Neiman with the same avidity that another curator was concurrently deaccessioning and disposing of that same artist's paintings. At best this would be confusing; at worst, self-defeating.

In a great university, the expression of a multiplicity of views may be a sign of open and healthy inquiry. At their current level of development, the same may not be true for museums. It might be taken instead as a sign of managerial disarray. While consistency need not be carried to every last detail, the successful operation of a museum today would still seem to require that it project some basic point of view, some over-arching set of values. A history museum that at one and the same time treated the American labor movement as a vital force for progress *and* as a quasi-criminal intrusion upon the rights of capital might forfeit any claim to be taken seriously. A contemporary art museum that accorded equal importance to the paintings of Jackson Pollack and of Norman Rockwell would be open to general ridicule.

If a consistent point of view is to be reflected, whose point of view should it be? For many of the world's museums, this is a simple question. These museums operate under ministries of culture or ministries of education. The point of view to be reflected is that of the government. In those instances where the government and a political party are virtually coextensive, then the line of that political party becomes the museum's mandatory point of view. In the German Democratic Republic, for example, the line that was dictated in 1972 by the ruling Socialist Unity Party provided that historical scholarship:

> takes as its point of departure that the socialist world system gathered around the Soviet Union is the inevitable result of the entire course of world history and that the GDR is the legitimate heir to all the revolutionary, progressive and humanistic traditions of German history and, above all, of the German workers movement.

To this day, the history museums of the GDR reflect just that point of view. Here, for example, is how East Berlin's Museum für Deutsche Geshichte—the Museum of German History—describes its overall program:

> As a socialist center of education, [the Museum] acquaints visitors with the revolutionary, democratic and humanist traditions of the

German people. It emphasizes the role of the masses as the real makers of history.

In the United States, by contrast, we have no centralized source of ideology for museums. Our thousands upon thousands of museums are independently governed. Even if we did have some inclination to make them all march in ideological lockstep, we lack any effective means to do it. Each museum will have its own point of view.

The question remains, though, as to who it is, within each museum, that is to establish this point of view—the board, the director, or the staff? We can, I think, rather quickly dispose of the possibility that it might be the staff. A museum is not a democracy. One of the director's principal roles is to direct the staff, not to represent it. His authority is delegated to him downward by the board, not conferred upon him upward by his staff acting in the manner of an electorate.

What of the board, then? Beyond question, a museum's board of trustees has the *authority* to establish the institution's point of view. The more pertinent question is whether it has the *competence* to do so—and to do so at any useful level of detail. Most often, board members will have been selected for their competence in some other field (law, finance, communications) or their access to desired resources (money, collections, local government) rather than for any detailed knowledge of the museum's subject matter. Moreover, the very size of many boards (as well as the procedures by which they operate) would render them highly ineffectual in formulating and reformulating a museum's point of view on any detailed and ongoing basis. At best, the board's role in the formulation of an institutional viewpoint is an indirect one. It is manifested through the board's designation and retention of a director.

This is not to diminish such a role. It may even be the single most important function that a board performs. It is not, though, the same as formulating ongoing substantive points of view on the wide variety of instances that may fall within the scope of the museum's subject matter. To paraphrase one commentator, the board's job is not to run a museum but, rather, to see to it that it *is* run.

In the end, then, it is to the director that we must look to establish a museum's particular truth, its point of view, even—if you will—its taste. While the conclusion may seem startling— and not at all a happy one for those who would prefer to see museums organized on some more collegial basis—it may well be that a museum operates best on that same hierarchical model as does the army, the church, and the traditional industrial corporation. This is a model in which decisions on matters of grave institutional importance—on matters, if you will, of faith and morals—are made at the top and disseminated downward. It is the director's great privilege—and his awesome responsibility as well—to determine the truths that a museum will tell and the beliefs that it will transmit.

But here, of course, is the catch. For the director to be effective, it is not sufficient that the points of view he brings to the museum be consistent. They must also be persuasive. The director, after all, does more than simply direct the staff and formulate the museum's various points of view. He also acts as its principal public spokesman. When he expresses a museum's point of view, he must do so in terms that can be broadly accepted as informed and authoritative by all of the museum's various constituencies. He must speak in terms that can command the respect of its board, its staff, its patrons, its visitors, its community, its commentators, and even its critics.

We return then to our initial question: which of them might be more effective as the director of a museum—a disciplinary specialist or a managerial generalist? While many arguments can be adduced on either side, it seems to me that a consideration of two of the roles that a director must play—those of formulating the museum's ideological stance and of acting as spokesman to disseminate that stance to the museum's several publics—tilt the balance conclusively in favor of the disciplinary specialist.

The managerial generalist cannot be expected to have the education or experience that would enable him successfully to formulate a consistent, persuasive, informed, and authoritative point of view with respect to the museum's subject matter. This task—as important, perhaps, as any in the museum—would of necessity have to be delegated to subordinate staff members. Neither could such a generalist necessarily be expected to act effectively as a spokesman with respect to the museum's subject matter. Again, his only choice—absent some talent in the use of cue cards—might be to delegate this duty to subordinates.

In the absence of a candidate who presents an ideal balance of disciplinary knowledge and managerial skills, those who select a museum director must choose between a disciplinary specialist prepared and able to learn the rudiments of management or a managerial generalist who either can quickly absorb the methods, ethics, literature, and value of a disciplinary field or who is otherwise prepared to delegate several key elements of his directorship to his subordinates. Considering this very alternative with respect to art museums, the Association of Art Museum Directors concluded in its 1978 report on training needs that "It makes more sense to train art historians to be managers than to train administrators—who are not naturally inclined toward the visual arts—to understand and be sympathetic to art or to comprehend the role of the museum."

A decade later, that conclusion still seems right.

DEACCESSION PRACTICES
IN AMERICAN MUSEUMS

A generation ago, the practice of systematically thinning out and refining museum collections was perceived by many observers—both among the public at large and within museums themselves—as at least questionable and quite possibly unethical. There was a sense that once an object had entered a museum collection it should be considered a permanent part of the public patrimony and could not subsequently be simply discarded or returned to what might have been its former status as private property. There was also a concern that if the object has been donated, its subsequent disposition might be construed as a breach of good faith to the donor.

This attitude no longer prevails. A review of the collections management policies and practices of major American museums of every discipline makes it clear that the adoption of some process for pruning and upgrading collections is now widely—if not universally—accepted as a routine part of good museum management. Given both the diversity and decentralization of the American system of museums, it should not be a surprise that there has not yet emerged any single point of view—nor even any single body of law—as to the criteria for determining which

Reprinted, with permission, from *Museum News*, February 1987. Copyright © 1987, American Association of Museums. All rights reserved.

objects may properly be removed from museum collections or, once removed, in what manner such objects are to be transferred, discarded, exchanged, sold, or otherwise disposed of. What has emerged is a common vocabulary with which to describe these processes: the verb *deaccession* has been coined to describe the permanent removal of an object from a museum collection; the verb *dispose* has been adopted to describe the action taken with respect to such an object following its removal.

WHO DEACCESSIONS?

It should be understood that the larger American context includes institutions that do not favor (or cannot legally engage in) deaccessioning and disposition. And there are many museum officials who believe that the removal of objects from collections has too often been undertaken without appropriate caution. The National Gallery of Art, for example—although technically empowered under its bylaws to deaccession any work in its collection[1]—deaccessions only works of graphic art that are "true duplicates" of other works in its collection. There are also American museums entirely prohibited from deaccessioning by the terms of their governing instruments or controlling legislation. These, however, appear to be rare. It would seem that the majority of museums in the United States can and do deaccession and consider it—in one museum director's words—"an essential process for a living museum in contrast to a library or repository."[2]

WHY DEACCESSION?

Among those museums that can and do actively engage in deaccessioning, three considerations seem paramount. First is the recognition that the retention of each and every object in a museum's collection involves an ongoing expense. To the extent that any portion of a museum's resources is absorbed by the care of objects considered of only secondary importance or no longer useful, then the care of objects of primary importance must to that same degree be neglected. Examples of objects no longer useful to a museum might include those that have become separated from their data or those so deteriorated that their repair would render them essentially false.

Addressing a museum conference at the Smithsonian Institution in 1983, Washington architect George E. Hartman, Jr., calculated that the annual cost to heat, cool, clean, and guard the space in which museum objects are stored was $25 per square foot and that the average object kept in storage occupied two square feet. To this annual expense must be added the initial cost to construct such space—Hartman calculated this at $215 per square foot—as well as the expenses of taking periodic inventories, maintaining records, and making condition surveys. Viewed from this perspective, it is possible to conclude that a museum may have a positive duty to disemburden itself from the care of objects that are of little or no value in carrying out its mission.

A second consideration is that deaccessioning may generate funds with which to acquire other and more desirable objects. Thus, when the Solomon R. Guggenheim Museum announced that its fifteen-year effort to purchase Constantin Brancusi's 1912 marble sculpture *The Muse* had finally succeeded, it also announced that the purchase price would be raised in part by sales from the museum's collection. In a similar vein, the Art Institute of Chicago recently sold two lesser works by Monet and several by Renoir to purchase two canvases from Monet's haystack series to add to the four already in its collection. In the words of its director, this enabled the Institute to become "the only place in the world where one can see these works in numbers adequate to convey Monet's original intention."[3]

Lastly, in some natural history museums, a specimen in a collection may be deaccessioned on the grounds that the discipline itself would be better served if the object in question was transferred to another museum. At the Santa Barbara Museum of

Natural History, for example, material may be deaccessioned "in response to the scientific, educational, or exhibit needs in another institution."[4] In 1985, acting under this policy, the museum gave twenty-nine thousand herbarium sheets to a local botanic garden that, in the museum's view, had a greater research interest in plants and a better collections facility in which to store this material. In 1984, for similar reasons, the Stanford Museum and Nature Center in Connecticut transferred the Hubbell Collection of some ninety thousand mollusks to the Delaware Museum of Natural History. Likewise, the American Museum of Natural History permits deaccessioning "when the interests of science can best be served by such actions."[5] At Chicago's Field Museum of Natural History, collection specimens may be transferred to other institutions when this is "deemed to be in the best interest of Field Museum and society."[6]

THE DEACCESSION PROCESS

Regardless of how aggressively a museum may hope to pursue a deaccession policy, there may nevertheless be objects in its collection—most frequently donated objects—that are subject to legal restrictions that prevent their disposition. Although current American museum practice discourages the acceptance of gifts that carry such restrictions, this was not always the case, nor are museums consistently successful in always avoiding such restrictions. Accordingly, the first step in the deaccessioning of any object must be an investigation of the circumstances under which it was acquired. For this, good records are essential. If no impediment appears, the museum may proceed with the deaccessioning process. If there is an impediment, the possibility remains that—in some instances—a legal way may be found to clear it away. Most frequently this would be done by a *cy pres* proceeding in a local court.[7]

Less clear-cut are those instances in which a donor has expressed a preference that an object not be deaccessioned (or, if it were to be deaccessioned, suggested how this should be done), but has not absolutely forbidden it. Such restrictions are generally described as *precatory*. Museums differ widely in their written policies with respect to precatory restrictions. Some are wholly silent, some provide that such restrictions should be observed for whichever is shorter of a specific period of years or the donor's lifetime, and some require that the museum make an effort to have such restrictions modified by the donor or, if the donor is no longer living, by the donor's heirs or legal representatives. Even with respect to donated objects to which no restrictions apply, museum policies differ widely as to whether and, if so, under what circumstances, the donor or his heirs must, at the very least, be notified of a pending deaccession.

Once it is determined that an object *can* be deaccessioned, the next question becomes whether it *should* be. It is here that those who advise extreme caution with respect to deaccessioning most often make their strongest case. Their fear is that the selection of objects may be arbitrary, capricious, and subject either to the vagaries of fashion or to the poorly informed judgment of a board of trustees. Some number of horror stories may be told of museums that have made what appear to be serious mistakes in their choice of objects to deaccession. One of the most widely experienced American museum directors—now retired—has called it a "crime" for "those controlling a public museum to confuse their personal taste with critical judgment."[8]

In response to this concern, those museums that do deaccession increasingly do so under tightly written procedures intended to assure that their decisions in this area will be subject to scrupulous review and consultation. In recent years, procedures have generally appeared in collections management policies intended to describe "the goals of a museum and explain how these goals are pursued through collection activity."[9] Clearly, no museum can determine what is extrinsic to its purposes until it can identify its true purposes.

Under the procedure followed by the Smithsonian Institution's National Museum of American History, for example, the initial inquiry as to whether an object may be considered for deaccession poses the following questions:[10]

- Is the object no longer relevant and useful to the purpose and activities of the museum?
- Is there danger of not being able to preserve the object properly?
- Has the object deteriorated beyond usefulness?
- Is it doubtful that the object can be used in the foreseeable future?
- Will this deaccession provide the means for improving or strengthening the collections in order to further the goals of the museum?

By contrast, the Chicago Museum of Science and Industry—a museum in which constructed education exhibits are emphasized over any collection of artifacts—employs a single criterion: materials from its collections may be sold, transferred, or discarded if they are no longer of value to the museum.[11]

WHO DECIDES?

Who is to make such a determination? *Professional Practices in Art Museums*, the report of the ethics and standards committee of the Association of Art Museum Directors, suggests that the procedure for deaccessioning should be at least as rigorous as that for making major acquisitions. In some museums it is more so. In most museums, the final approval for *every* deaccession must be made by the board of trustees or other governing body based on recommendations both by the director of the museum and the curator responsible for the care of the object. In others, the level at which the decision is made may turn upon the value of the object in question. Field Museum of Natural History permits transfers of less than $1,000 on the recommendation of a curator, with final approval by the department chairman. If the value is above $1,000 but below $10,000, the approval of the director is also required. If the value is $10,000 or more, the board of trustees must also approve.

Virtually universal is some system of checks and balances aimed at preventing the process from proceeding capriciously as well as some requirement that there be curatorial approval of any proposed disposition. To estimate an object's value—which may, in turn, indicate the level of approval that will be required in order to deaccession it—collections management policies frequently require one or more outside appraisals.

DISPOSITION

Once the competent authority has determined that an object both *can* and *should* be deaccessioned and the necessary formalities have been observed—most typically, if trustee approval is required, this consists of an entry in the board's minutes recording the action taken—the question then arises of how to dispose of the object. Depending upon the reason for its deaccession, the answer to this may or may not be implicit. If, for example, the object was deaccessioned because it had deteriorated beyond usefulness, it might simply be discarded. If it was deaccessioned because it might be more suitable for another institution, then it might be transferred to that institution.

More complex considerations may arise when the object to be disposed of has a substantial market value. This is most typically the case with art museums. Which is the museum's duty: to assure the future welfare of—and public accessibility to—the object by assuring that it passes to another museum or public institution? Or to maximize for itself the proceeds to be received from a sale to the highest bidder? Here, conflicting views exist.

On the one side is a resolution concerning deaccessioning adopted by the College Art Association—a national organization composed principally of scholars, artists, and art museum curators—which includes the following paragraph: "If the work to be removed from a collection would be a desirable acquisition for another public institution, full consideration should be given to making the work directly available for acquisition by such an institution."[12]

The published guidelines of the New York State Association of Museums take a similar position. Discussing the disposition of deaccessioned material, the guidelines state: "Consideration should be given to placing the objects, through gift, exchange, or sale, in another tax-exempt public institution wherein they may serve the purpose for which they were acquired initially."[13]

It may, however, be argued that such an approach would involve the trustees of the disposing institution in a violation of their fiduciary duty. If the other public institution was prepared to purchase the object for 4x dollars while a potential private purchaser would pay 6x, what are the trustees to do? Or further, if the other public institution willing to pay 4x is in a remote and distant community—or even a foreign country—but another museum in their same locality is willing to pay 3x, what are they to do? So long as their primary duty is to their own museum, the answers seem clear. Once they begin to acquire some vague duty to institutions elsewhere, though, these answers become muddy.

At least one major art museum—the Metropolitan Museum of Art, which has a history of deaccessioning and disposition that dates back to 1885—has taken a position contrary to the College Art Association's. Its policy statement on deaccessioning notes that the museum's trustees "would not wish to be bound to the limitations imposed by limiting sales or exchanges to other museums. Their primary duty is to the Metropolitan and its constituencies. Not all museums are in a position to make large cash purchases and some have little to exchange."[14]

In a similar vein, at Field Museum of Natural History, the decision to sell deaccessioned material has only a single goal: "To

Preface

Deaccessioning is a bold move which no museum undertakes lightly. After careful deliberation, the Corcoran Gallery of Art has decided to sell at public auction 100 works from its collection of European paintings. Funds generated by this sale will be placed in a separate, restricted account designated solely for the purchase of American art of historical importance.

As Director of the Corcoran, I look upon this action as a means of keeping the museum's identity clear and focused, as a way of defining its mission and planning for its future, and as a method of improving its collections. From its establishment in 1869, the Corcoran has enjoyed a pre-eminent position in the field of American art. This sale will permit the Gallery—a private institution with very limited funds for acquisition—to fill some of the major lacunae in its outstanding American collection, without diminishing the effectiveness of the institution.

Conscious of its responsibility to donors and mindful of its obligation to the public, the Corcoran followed rigorous procedures in selecting the objects for this sale. From curatorial recommendation to final Board approval, each work was carefully scrutinized and its relevance to the Gallery's present and future programs weighed. It was decided that the works should be sold at auction to insure that they were offered to the largest possible audience. Trustees and staff of the Gallery, and members of their immediate families, are restricted from bidding on these paintings.

Several of the works offered for sale were given to the Corcoran with the expressed purpose that they be sold and American works purchased with the resultant funds. In the case of the European paintings owned by William Wilson Corcoran, the donor himself (in what is an extraordinary example of farsighted museum philanthropy) stipulated in his deed of gift that their disposition was at the discretion of the Trustees. Donors of works sold will be acknowledged in future publications and on identifying labels for the works of art purchased through their generous gifts.

It is hoped that this sale will help make a great museum of American art even greater. And it is in this spirit and with this intention that we have taken this important step.

DR. PETER C. MARZIO
Director
Corcoran Gallery of Art

On May 3, 1979, the Corcoran Gallery of Art sold 100 nineteenth-century European paintings from its collection through public auction at Sotheby Parke Bernet in New York City. The preface to the auction catalogue, above, stands as an excellent summary of the considerations that should be taken into account in a successful deaccession—successful both in its consequences for a refined and upgraded collection and successful in its positive impact on the museum's reputation.

bring the best possible price for the material being sold."[15] Only when the museum receives substantially equivalent offers can one purchaser be preferred over another on the grounds that it might be a more appropriate depository for the material.

If sale is decided upon as the means to dispose of deaccessioned objects, then the choice must still be made between a negotiated private sale and a public auction. While most collections management policies permit either method, there is a strong preference today for public auction—at least for those objects for which an auction market exists. As the Metropolitan Museum of Art discovered in the early 1970s when the *New York Times* took issue with certain dispositions made from its collection, private sales run the risk that suspicions may arise over the way a price was determined or as to whether all potential purchasers were given an equal opportunity to buy. Whatever its flaws, public auction appears to be the most satisfactory means to sell most objects of value disposed of by museums. It should be noted, incidentally, that almost all collections management policies provide that neither museum employees nor officers nor trustees may be the purchasers of deaccessioned museum objects offered either through private sale or public auction.

Objects to be disposed of by public auction are most frequently consigned to mixed-owner sales at as important an auction house as the material will permit. On rare occasions, however, a museum may choose to hold a single-owner sale. In at least one recent instance—the disposition in 1985 by the Henry Ford Museum and Greenfield Village of some four hundred "redundant or out-of-scope objects"—such an auction was actually conducted on the museum's own premises.

APPLICATION OF PROCEEDS

Almost without exception, collections management policies require that the proceeds from the sale of any deaccessioned objects be used for the benefit of the collection. Most frequently such funds are to be used for acquisition; in some instances they may be used instead to construct or improve storage areas. Without some such restriction, though, it is doubtful that curators would ever be willing to recommend any deaccessions whatsoever. Moreover, many regard such a restriction as essential to preventing governing boards or other ruling authorities from looking to a museum's collection as a potential source of operating funds.

In some instances, the requirements as to the application of funds are cast in the broadest possible terms. Thus, the policy of the Brooklyn Museum simply requires that "proceeds from the sale of deaccessioned objects will be used for the purchase of works of art for the curatorial department from which the objects came."[16]

By contrast, the Philadelphia Museum of Art's policy is fairly elaborate: "The proceeds of all sales should go into an acquisitions fund, and efforts should be made to replace a work of art with one or more of approximately equal value for which it was sold to reflect the donor's interests, and to bear the name of the donor of the object sold."[17]

Most other collections management policies contain similar language requiring that a donor's name be carried over to the replacement object acquired.

PUBLIC REGULATION

To the best of my knowledge, there are not currently any state or local laws that regulate deaccessioning by privately governed American museums. In New York State, however—and possibly elsewhere—there have been intermittent attempts over the past decade to enact such legislation. Basically, these proposed enactments would not affect the freedom to deaccession that these museums now enjoy. They would, rather, establish stricter recordkeeping requirements, provide for greater public access to museum records, and, in some instances, require advance public notice of a museum's intention to deaccession. Some or all of these requirements also appear in a series of voluntary arrangements entered into by the New York State attorney general's office and several New York City museums in which past deaccessioning practices had been the subject of controversy.

Notwithstanding a lack of specific legislation, it is nonetheless within the power of most state attorneys general to bring a legal proceeding against the trustees of a museum that is believed to be deaccessioning objects from its collection imprudently or for improper purposes. An example involving allegations of imprudence is that of the Maryhill Museum in Klickitat County, Washington. There, the attorney general commenced an action in 1977 seeking to remedy a situation in which, among other things, valuable museum objects were being traded for worthless substitutes.[18] The action was less than wholly successful in terms of restoring any of the museum's lost property.

A more encouraging result was obtained in Chicago where the attorney general was able to prevent the George F. Harding Museum from proceeding with a series of deaccessions that were intended primarily to raise funds to be paid as salaries to members of its board of trustees.[19] While this case, litigated for nearly a decade, is still in its final phases [it was finally settled in 1989], the Harding Museum's collection has meanwhile been salvaged and transferred in its entirety to the Art Institute of Chicago.

CONCLUSION

A deaccession process that is murky, secretive, and seemingly arbitrary may still today—no less so than a generation ago—appear to the public as at least questionable and quite possibly unethical. Approached sensibly, however, and protected by thoroughly worked-out procedural safeguards, the establishment and pursuit of a clearly articulated deaccession policy may be among the most vital practices that a museum can adopt for its own well-being and the well-being of the community that supports it. As a veteran art museum director has phrased it: "Under the private system governing nonprofit organizations, a museum must be considered an organism that develops from within. As it grows and expands it must also adapt to new conditions. It cannot perpetually take in without also giving out. Deaccessioning, that is, the continuous process of defining, upgrading, and removing, therefore seems to me to be an entirely normal and desirable process."[20]

The logic appears inescapable. For those museums that collect in "open" fields, i.e., those in which new objects are constantly being created—history, technology, and contemporary art are all examples—the only alternatives to deaccessioning are to accept the expense of continually increasing storage facilities, maintenance budgets, and staff, or else to cease collecting entirely. The first may be impractical. The second would be irresponsible. By contrast, the adoption of a soundly based deaccession policy is both practical and responsible.

Notes

1. Article XIII, Section 4. Except for duplicate prints, a two-thirds vote of the entire membership of the board of trustees is required.

2. Letter from the director of the Art Institute of Chicago to the author, dated January 10, 1986.

3. See note 2 above.

4. *Santa Barbara Museum of Natural History Collections Policy,* September 7, 1984.

5. American Museum of Natural History, *A Statement of Policy and Procedures Regulating the Acquisition and Disposition of Natural History Specimens,* April 1974.

6. Field Museum of Natural History, *Policy Statement on Accessions and Deaccessions,* dated November 17, 1975.

7. *cy pres:* the doctrine in the law of charities whereby when it becomes impossible, impracticable, or illegal to carry out the particular purpose of the donor a scheme will be framed by a court to carry out the general intention by applying the gift to charitable purposes that are closely related or similar to the original purposes.

8. Letter from Charles Parkhurst to the author, January 15, 1986.

9. Marie C. Malaro, *A Legal Primer on Managing Museum Collections* (Washington, D.C.: Smithsonian Institution Press, 1986): 43.

10. Smithsonian Institution, *National Museum of American History Collections Management Policy,* February 1, 1984.

11. Museum of Science and Industry, *Administrative Order No. 10,* February 25, 1981.

12. College Art Association, "The Sale and Exchange of Works of Art by Museums," a resolution, November 3, 1973.

13. New York State Association of Museums, *The Ethics and Responsibilities of Museums with Respect to the Acquisition and Disposition of Collection Materials,* April 1974.

14. Metropolitan Museum of Art, "Report on Art Transactions, 1971–73."

15. See note 6 above.

16. Brooklyn Museum, *Policy Guidelines for Accessioning and Deaccessioning by Action of the Board of Governors,* June 14, 1978.

17. Philadelphia Museum of Art, *Deaccessioning Policy and Procedure,* June 13, 1979.

18. State of Washington ex rel. *Gordon* v. *Leppaluoto, et al.,* Nos. 11777 and 11781 (Superior Court, Klickitat Co., Wash., 1977). For a history of the museum and its problems, see Patricia Failing, "The Maryhill Museum: A Case History of Cultural Abuse," *ARTnews,* (March 1977): 83–90.

19. People ex rel. *Scott* v. *Silverstein, et al.,* No. 76 CH 6446 (Circuit Court, Cook County, Ill., County Dept., Chancery Div., October 28, 1976).

20. Letter from the director of the Solomon R. Guggenheim Museum to the author, January 7, 1986.

DEACCESSIONING MODERN
AND CONTEMPORARY ART

Some Notes on the American
Experience

I n a typical acerbic annotation to *The Works
of Sir Joshua Reynolds,* William Blake ob-
served, "To Generalize is to be an Idiot. To Particularize is the
Alone Distinction of Merit."

Blake's observation holds true for museums. Generaliza-
tions about museums most often miss the mark. The general
question of how a museum ought best manage its collection—no
less the more critical inquiry as to what sort of policy it should
adopt with respect to deaccessioning—cannot begin to be addressed without reference to the particular kind of a museum that
it is. While virtually every museum is, to a degree, engaged in the
three core functions of preservation, study, and public communication, the relative emphasis that it gives to each of those functions may vary markedly from one institution to another.

For the museum that is chiefly depository or archival—one
that takes its principal mission to be the preservation of specimens and artifacts that might otherwise be lost to posterity—the
issue of deaccessioning will scarcely arise. If to preserve more
examples of something is simply considered more worthwhile
than to preserve fewer, then the very notion of refining its collec-

Published as "Deaccessioning in American Museums: I," in *Apollo* magazine, 130 (330 new series), August 1989.

tion must *per se* be antithetical to such a museum's basic vision of its mandate. That would hold true as well for any museum initially established not for some living purpose but to serve as a static memorial or shrine.

Deaccessioning might be equally inappropriate for the museum that makes scholarship its primary goal. The fact that an object may no longer be suitable for public display might be irrelevant in terms of its potential for research. Likewise, the fact that an object might be duplicative or otherwise redundant would not necessarily diminish its utility: similar objects might, for example, be usefully subjected to dissimilar forms of investigation.

For the museum that is fundamentally devoted to public communication, however—and in the United States, at least, that would include most museums of modern and contemporary art—the situation is different. The collection of such a museum is neither intended principally to be an end in itself nor to serve primarily as a subject for research. The collection of such a museum has been gathered and is maintained for the purpose of public education. Periodically to shape and reshape such a collection in order that it may better serve the museum's purpose—to rid the collection of objects which, although relatively useless to its needs, continue to drain the museum of the resources required for their care—may be more than merely permissible or appropriate. In such a museum, the process of shaping and reshaping its collection, of pruning and winnowing to the end that the collection may be upgraded and supplemented, might well be the hallmark of a sound, dynamic, and farsighted approach to collections management.

More and more, American art museums are deaccessioning what they consider to be superfluous or redundant works of art. This can be clearly seen by examining the catalogues of the major auction houses. Last autumn's sales in New York, for example, included paintings and sculpture consigned to auction by the Art Institute of Chicago, the Baltimore Museum of Art, the Sterling and Francine Clark Institute, and the Hirshhorn Museum and

Sculpture Garden. Other recent auctions have included works of art consigned by, among others, the Museum of Modern Art, the St. Louis Art Museum, the Metropolitan Museum of Art, the Phillips Collection, the Whitney Museum of American Art, and the Los Angeles County Museum of Art.

That American art museums may today feel less hesitant than formerly with respect to such deaccessioning should not, however, suggest that such a practice has developed wholly without constraints or that it can be pursued willy-nilly. On the contrary, a number of rules, some formal, others less so, have accumulated around this practice. Perhaps the most important of these is that a museum must use the proceeds from deaccessioning to benefit its collection. This is specifically laid down in paragraph 27 of *Professional Practices in Art Museums,* the guide to ethics and standards first promulgated by the Association of Art Museum Directors (AAMD) in 1971. This provides that:

> The deaccession and disposal of a work of art from a museum's collection requires particularly rigorous examination. Deaccessioning should be related to policy rather than to the exigencies of the moment, and funds obtained through disposal must be used to replenish the collection.

In several recent instances, institutions that proposed to use the sales proceeds from deaccessioned objects for other purposes have been persuaded to change their plans in whole or in part, when the AAMD took the position that to do so would constitute a "breach of principle." This was the case when Harvard proposed, late in 1981, to deaccession works of art from its Fogg Art Museum in order to raise operating funds for what was to be a new wing for the museum. Faced with a formal statement of condemnation, Harvard initially cancelled the new wing entirely. When this produced an even greater storm of protest, the university found other means to construct and maintain the new wing.

A more recent instance involved the Phillips Collection in Washington, D.C. In 1987, the Phillips announced that it had deaccessioned and planned to sell *Le Violon,* a 1914 Cubist painting by Georges Braque, a work that Marcel Duchamp had personally selected for the collector Katherine S. Dreier in 1924 and which Ms. Dreier, in turn, had bequeathed to the Phillips at her death in 1952. The proceeds were to be added to the Phillips' general endowment. Once again, the AAMD, referring to its code of professional practices, pointed out that to use the proceeds in this manner would violate the standards it had promulgated for art museums.

While the Phillips ultimately did proceed with the sale—*Le Violon* was auctioned at Sotheby's in New York on November 11, 1987, for $3,000,000 plus the 10 percent buyer's premium—it agreed to a compromise on the proposed use of the moneys it received. These, it said, would be kept together as a fund for future acquisitions. Whatever income was generated pending such use would be applied exclusively to the care and maintenance of the permanent collection.

Another rule almost universally observed is that, notwithstanding that the approval of its board of trustees or other governing body will ultimately be required, the impetus for deaccessioning should initially come from those most immediately responsible for a museum's collection, i.e., from its curatorial staff and director. This is consistent with the rationale that deaccessioning should be employed solely to benefit the museum's collection, not in order to help it meet its operating budget. In the catalogue for a 1982 auction of some seven hundred works of art and other objects sold by the Los Angeles County Museum of Art "to benefit new acquisitions," its director gave the following description of that museum's deaccessioning process:

> So that it may . . . maintain the level of quality expected by a community which is expanding rapidly in knowledge and sophistication, the Museum unceasingly reviews and studies all works of art in its possession, periodically subjecting them to strict scrutiny

to determine their condition, their art historical importance, their value to the permanent collection, and their utility to the community ... The criteria for deaccessioning are many: an artist or culture may be represented by more important examples; the Museum may have a large number of objects of one type or period and be entirely lacking in representation of other types or periods; or some works may no longer meet the standard of quality which rises as the collection grows.

A further self-imposed restriction in some museums—the Hirshhorn Museum is one—discourages the deaccessioning of work by a living artist without the artist's prior approval. At the Museum of Modern Art a similar policy extends to American artists only. Such policies are intended, out of common courtesy, to protect the artist's livelihood. Exceptions might be made—the Hirshhorn has made several: it did, for example, dispose at auction of a duplicate cast of Henry Moore's large *Seated Woman* in May 1986, several months before the sculptor's death—but only when the artist's reputation and market appear so secure that such a transaction should not cause these any damage.

The predominant practice among American museums is to channel the proceeds from deaccessioned works of art into their general acquisitions funds. In a few museums, however, such funds may be earmarked for an even more narrow purpose. At the Philadelphia Museum of Art, for example, curators are urged to replace a deaccessioned work of art with one of approximately equal value that might continue to carry the name as well as reflect the interests of the original donor.

In other museums, this procedure is reversed by having the acquisition decision *precede* the deaccessioning one. If the funds to acquire an important object are to be raised through deaccessioning, then this second approach often requires that the works chosen to be deaccessioned should be as close in period and medium as may be practical to the work to be acquired. Thus, in order to acquire two paintings from Claude Monet's haystack series, the Art Institute of Chicago sold two lesser works by

Monet as well as several others by Pierre-Auguste Renoir. In a similar vein, when the Solomon R. Guggenheim Museum acquired its marble version of Constantin Brancusi's 1912 sculpture, *The Muse,* in 1985, the funds to cover its cost were raised in part by selling a plaster version of *The Muse* acquired some years earlier. Also sold were what the Museum considered to be lesser works by several other important sculptors of the period including Raymond Duchamp-Villon and Jacques Lipchitz. Likewise, to help underwrite its 1987 purchase of *Seguidilla,* a key 1919 work in mixed media by Man Ray, the Hirshhorn Museum and Sculpture Garden deaccessioned a group of other works by the same artist that the director and curatorial staff had judged to be relatively less significant.

While auction sales have become the primary means through which most museums dispose of deaccessioned works of art, occasions may arise when a mutually beneficial exchange can be arranged. A dramatic instance of this occurred in 1982 when the Museum of Modern Art surrendered important paintings by Pablo Picasso and Henri Matisse to the Guggenheim in exchange for two paintings by Wassily Kandinsky. Through this exchange, the Modern was able to complete the ensemble of Kandinsky's four-painting suite, *Four Seasons,* while the Guggenheim was, at the same time, able to fill certain gaps in its collection. As the two museums noted in a joint press release: "The exchange importantly strengthens the collection of each of the institutions with works by artists particularly well represented in the other."

Notwithstanding that deaccessioning has been able to produce such salutary results in American art museums, it still continues to encounter resistance. On what is this based? The arguments that it might constitute a breach of faith with past donors or discourage present ones do not seem persuasive. Restrictions placed upon their gifts by donors have legal consequences that museums cannot ignore. The first step in any deaccessioning process must always be to determine whether the work in question may be disposed of in a legally acceptable manner. If not, the process ends right there. As for present donors, the anecdotal evidence to date would tend to indicate that a well-managed programme of deaccessioning, one that is clear, purposeful, and conducted with integrity, is just as likely to make a museum attractive to donors as otherwise.

Of greater weight is the argument of "fallibility"—that those responsible for deaccessioning a work of art may ultimately prove to have been mistaken, either as to the facts of its authorship or, more likely, in their judgment as to its quality or importance. While the possibility of factual error is real enough for museums with collections of earlier art—the specter most commonly raised is that of the carelessly discarded Renaissance painting which, to the deaccessioning museum's utter and everlasting humiliation, subsequently turns out to have been from the hand of Leonardo da Vinci—it has little pertinence to modern or contemporary collections where questions of authorship rarely arise. Not so, however, with errors of judgment. These are a real and haunting possibility for every museum that deaccessions. Although such errors can never be wholly avoided, much can be done to minimize them. A good starting point is another of the standards promulgated by the AAMD—that the procedure for the deaccession of a work of art be "at least as rigorous" as that for the acquisition of one. In most American museums, it is even more so. Decisions to deaccession are, to the extent possible, made through a broad, deliberately paced and informed consensus, not hastily or by individual fiat. Moreover, if a deaccessioned work is to be disposed of by public sale, this fact is generally given broad advance publicity in order that dissenting views can come to the surface. Also widely observed is a principle that has long been enshrined in the Museum of Modern Art's formal deaccessioning policy: that work of art must never be sold simply because the artist who created it is currently "out of fashion."

What must be understood in the end, however, is that it is exactly the same people that have been entrusted to build museum collections through selective acquisitions who are also responsible for the refining of those same collections through selective dispositions. If their judgment is considered trustworthy in the case of *accessioning*—if their perceptions of quality and importance are what a museum relies upon to commit its slender and very precious acquisitions funds—then why should there be such skepticism about their judgment in the case of *deaccessioning*?

During a lively debate over deaccessioning practices conducted at the 1987 meeting of the Council of Australian Museum Associations in Brisbane, it was the forceful reiteration of exactly this question by Patrick McCaughey—then director of the National Gallery of Victoria, now director of the Wadsworth Atheneum in Hartford, Connecticut—that carried the day against the "fallibility" argument advanced by the opposing side. In a similar vein, one veteran American museum official recently noted: "It is the same eyes that sell well or poorly as those that buy well or poorly. The director or curator who does not know how to sell probably does not know how to buy."

Errors of commission are potentially inherent in any program of deaccessioning. Those who focus on that possibility rarely discuss, however, the equal potential for errors of omission that is inherent in the process of acquiring. In theory, it should make no difference to the ultimate shape of a museum's collection if an important work of art was never purchased at all or if, having once been purchased, it was thereafter sold through poor judgment. Either way, the museum is without it.

In actual fact, however, the number of important art works that have failed ever to enter a museum's collection because somebody, whether for lack of judgment, opportunity, courage, or the necessary funds, failed to buy them in the first place must exceed by many a dozen the number of important art works that have been removed from such collections because somebody disposed of them in error. While deaccessioning is not without its dangers, we have found—in America, at least, and at least for museums of modern and contemporary art—that the risks it poses are not unmanageable and that the rewards it offers can be very great.

TOO MUCH ART?

In its basic sense, "triage"—from the French *trier,* to choose—simply means to sort or to sift. More common today, though—and more doom-laden, too—is the special sense it has acquired in the practice of battle-field medicine. In the face of a scarce resource—available medical assistance—"triage" has come to mean that grim decision process by which it is determined who among the wounded may be given the chance to live and who, out of necessity, must be left most likely to die.

During a symposium sponsored by ArtTable in New York this past January, I happened to suggest, virtually *en passant,* that the outpouring of newly made art in the United States was of such a magnitude that not all of it could possibly be preserved. Whether by selective neglect or deliberate destruction, it may sooner or later be necessary to practice some form of triage. So astonished, if not outraged, were a number of listeners that some further elaboration would seem in order.

How much art *are* we producing? To begin with, we need to know the number of visual artists currently at work in the United States. A widely used approximation is that projected by the

ARTnews, 88 (10), October 1989. This was originally written as column for the magazine's "Perspective" series.

federal Bureau of Labor Statistics for the occupational category of "painters, sculptors, craft-artists and artist printmakers." For 1988, this figure stood at 215,000. If we decrease it somewhat to eliminate the category of craft-artists but add something back to cover those other painters, sculptors, and artist printmakers whose income was primarily derived from teaching or some other non-art-making activity, then a current estimate of 200,000 working artists would appear conservative.

More difficult to calculate is their average output. How many works of art—from a casual sketch nonetheless deemed worthy of preservation to a wholly finished painting or sculpture—does an artist produce annually? The range, of course, must be enormous. Painters, sculptors, and printmakers all differ in their studio practices. Some artists work full-time, some only part. Artists of an expressionist tendency might well be more productive than those of a neo-plastic bent. Somewhere, nonetheless, is an average. Based on conversations with artists, an estimate of forty does not seem excessive.

Multiplying this last number by an estimate of two hundred thousand working artists, an annual production of eight million works of art can then be projected for this country alone. The art market can absorb only a fraction of such an output. What then happens to the rest? During the artist's lifetime, it piles up in the studio. Thereafter, for a handful of successful artists—the Warhols and Rothkos, the Pollocks, Krasners, and Gottliebs—a posthumous charitable foundation may serve as an appropriate and dignified conduit through which to distribute the residue by sale or gift.

What, though, of the other 99 percent of artists? To what extent must their families or surviving friends care for their undistributed oeuvre—finished, half-finished, and scarcely begun? Are these works a burden that they are obligated to carry indefinitely? And, if so, with what diligence, at what emotional cost, with what outlay of funds for conservation, recordkeeping and storage, and unto what generation?

When this issue arose at the symposium, one participant speculated that this caretaker function might be a proper task for museums. Those who manage American museums would largely disagree. In most art museums today, the tendency is in precisely the contrary direction—toward the selective upgrade and refinement of collections and away from uncritical agglomeration. In taking this tack, museums have a strong economic motivation.

In 1983, the Washington architect George E. Hartman, Jr., calculated that—above and beyond the amortized expense of construction—it was then costing American museums approximately $25 per square foot per year to climate control, guard, and clean their storage areas. The average work in storage, he found, occupied two square feet. Thus, to store as few as one thousand extra works would have then required an expense of $50,000 annually. That figure would be higher today. Even if museums *were* willing to act as the repositories of last resort, there is no way they could raise the additional tens of millions of dollars it would cost annually to take care of the overwhelming mass of art for which the world has no apparent long-term need.

What are the alternatives? The most draconian might be vocational—simply to limit the number of artists that could be trained in any generation. Our art schools currently graduate many thousands each year. Restricting those prepared to practice a given profession to the anticipated level of market demand is not an unknown device, particularly in centrally planned economies. It seems doubtful, though, that such a strategy would be acceptable in the United States. More certain is the romantic vision it would engender—of authentic and misunderstood geniuses denied entry to training while hordes of hacks were meanwhile admitted.

More practical might be the establishment of a some publicly supported facility in which an artist's otherwise undistributed work might be deposited. Through periodic exhibitions and auctions, whatever could find a buyer might be sold over time to help defray the facility's expenses. Whatever works could not be sold might be transferred to such museums, schools, hospitals, and other public institutions as chose to receive and take care of them. For the rest—in contrast to a museum—heroic preservation measures would be avoided. What nobody wanted would, after appropriate documentation, ultimately be allowed to perish through neglect.

Most practical of all, though, might be an attitudinal change. What must be reversed is the process by which art has been sacralized. So long as we treat every work of art—from the consensus masterpiece to the clearly most puerile—with indiscriminate reverence, then to that same extent the purposeful destruction of that art—whether by acts of omission or commission—must seem to us a profanation.

Not every novel is *War and Peace*. Not every symphony is Beethoven's Ninth. Historic preservation, at even its most extravagant, has never envisioned that every building can or ought be saved. The wise management of our art resources requires that we develop some clearer sense of their range of values than our current attitude allows. "Art," after all, is only a noun. The adjectives used to modify it can range from "sublime" to "superfluous." To acknowledge the reality of the latter might be a sound first step in approaching what can for the nonce—pending the evolution of some euphemism—only be described as an art glut.

THE MUSEUM
MANAGEMENT INSTITUTE

Its Genesis and Early Years

It makes more sense to train art historians to be managers than to train administrators—who are not naturally inclined toward the visual arts—to understand and be sympathetic to art or to comprehend the role of the museum (from the Association of Art Museum Directors' Report on Training Needs for Museum Directors, 1978).

The Museum Management Institute (MMI) is a four-week residential training program in museum management and business practices for mid-level and senior staff members from museums of all disciplines. Conducted annually during the last three weeks of July and the first week of August on the Berkeley campus of the University of California, MMI is a program activity of the J. Paul Getty Trust and is administered by the Art Museum Association of America (AMAA) with the University Extension, University of California, Berkeley (UCB).

MMI had its genesis in the mid-1970s, a period when the increasing scale and complexity of American museums were raising fears that they might no longer be susceptible to management by those who, like most curators and educators, had no more than the customary training in art history, the natural sciences, or other museum-related disciplines. Compounding this was a sense that the economic, legal, and social environments in which museums operated were becoming increasingly difficult. The competition for resources had grown more intense and there appeared to be a drift toward ever-closer scrutiny and more extensive public regulation. The apprehension was that boards of trustees might ultimately conclude that they needed to reach beyond the traditional museum community to bring in—either as directors or, under some newly designed two-headed staff structure, as co-directors—individuals with extensive backgrounds in business, diplomacy, the military, or other "wordly" pursuits. Within the rank and file of museum employees, this was viewed as a potential calamity. Among the strategies considered for countering it was the notion that experienced museum professionals might themselves—through programs of intense and accelerated training—acquire some of the management skills necessary for effective leadership of their institutions. While Harvard University had offered such training since 1971 through its annual summer Institute of Arts Administration (a program it was to continue through 1978), this was designed as much or more for the staffs of performing arts organizations. The experiences of those from museums who had attended were often disappointing.

One of the people who had given considerable thought to how a training program specific to museum professionals might be developed was Virginia Stern, until 1971 the curator in charge of education at the Detroit Institute of Arts. Following her move to California where her husband had been appointed dean of the University Extension at UCB (and following, also, her proposal of such a program to the Association of Art Museum Directors, who received it cordially but took no action), Ms. Stern approached the AMAA—then the Western Association of Art Museums (WAAM)—to suggest that they collaborate in seeking funds to develop a curriculum. Linda Evans, who was then in charge of coordinating WAAM's educational programs, was particularly responsive. She herself had recently attended the Harvard Institute of Arts Administration and had come to believe that a training program tailored closely to the needs of museum professionals would be more effective than the broader model which Harvard was then offering.

In 1976, Ms. Stern and Ms. Evans requested a planning grant from the National Endowment for the Arts (NEA), the independent federal agency established by the United States Congress in 1965 to foster the excellence, diversity, and vitality of the arts and to help broaden their availability and appreciation. This grant was awarded through WAAM, and a first planning meeting for what was to become MMI was held in Seattle, Washington, in June 1977. In July, a second meeting followed at Mills College in Oakland, California. The recommendations made at these first two meetings were generally accepted by WAAM and became the armature around which MMI was subsequently to develop.

The recommendations agreed on at the first planning meeting dealt chiefly with the eligibility of participants. Notwithstanding that WAAM's institutional membership consisted solely of art museums (and, at that time, only of art museums located west of the Mississippi River; as AMAA, it is now a national organization), it was recommended that the projected program be open, without geographic limitation, to staff members from museums of every discipline as well as from such related organizations as zoological parks, aquariums, and botanical gardens. To qualify for admission, the committee recommended that an applicant must have completed a minimum of four years of museum work, be currently employed by a museum, and be able to demonstrate institutional support for his or her attendance, preferably through employer-paid tuition but at least through salary continuation. Like the Harvard Institute of Arts Administration, it was proposed that the program be residential and scheduled to run for four weeks, but that the classes should be smaller. Initially it was recommended that these be limited to thirty participants. For budget reasons, this figure was later increased to thirty-five. Finally, the committee urged that every effort be made to provide a substantial pool of scholarship funds to assist participants in meeting their tuition fees, subsistence costs, and transportation.

Also recommended at that first planning meeting was that a university affiliation be given to the program. This, it was thought, would enhance both its credibility and its visibility. Given Ms. Stern's contact with UCB, which had expressed some previous interest, and given also that the UCB campus included three major museums (the Lawrence Hall of Science, the Robert H. Lowie Museum of Anthropology, and the University Art Museum), it seemed the ideal first choice. In due course, the UCB University Extension agreed to provide a site for the program (the library of the Men's Faculty Club, a 1900 Bernard Maybeck building), and to award continuing education units and certificates upon the course's completion. It also assisted in procuring the use of a university sorority house—otherwise unoccupied in summer—to serve as the program's residence and in arranging for participants to have access to the UCB's health clinic and its extensive recreational facilities.

At the second of these planning meetings, the focus was on the curriculum and faculty structure. Almost from the start, it was agreed that the curriculum should not include any "museological" topics such as conservation, collections management, or interpretation. Given the few classroom hours that would be available (less than 140), the availability elsewhere of courses covering these topics, and the presumed experience of the expected participants and the diversity of disciplines from which they would come, it appeared more useful to concentrate instruction on the two areas which the planning group had identified as most critical and which would be common to all the participants: human resources management and financial management. It was recommended that approximately 75 percent of instructional time be allotted to these. The balance was to be used for a variety of topics clustered around the nodes of governance, information management, the external environment, and professional standards. This in fact became the curriculum with which MMI began.

A major complaint about the Harvard Institute of Arts Administration had been the absence from its teaching staff of any practitioners with actual experience of working in arts organizations. Museum professionals who had attended the Harvard program complained that there were no senior members of the field available with whom they could discuss on an ongoing basis the practical relevance of management theories they were being taught. To rectify this, the planning group recommended a three-tier structure that would incorporate practicing museum professionals as a critical element.

At the top of this structure would be a director who would be in residence throughout the full four weeks and serve as a linking element for the various curriculum units. He or she was envisioned as coming from the world of continuing education and possessing teaching and counseling skills as well as having experience in the design and administration of institutes, conferences, and seminars. Working with the director would be four co-directors—to avoid confusion, this title was subsequently changed to senior museum associate—who would each serve for one week. They would be expected both to teach and to assist in interpreting the materials presented by the management faculty. To be sought as senior museum associates were museum directors or department heads from museums of different disciplines with at least fifteen to twenty years of experience and solid reputations within the profession. Finally, to complete this structure, there would be a management faculty, drawn chiefly from business schools and consulting firms, chosen for its subject-matter expertise rather than any particular familiarity with museums. With but two changes—the addition of an associate director to assist the director and of a financial management associate to take overall charge of the financial topics within the curriculum—this faculty structure has proven satisfactory and remains unchanged.

A final task of that second planning meeting was to recommend a name for the proposed program. After winnowing a good number, "Museum Management Institute" was finally proposed and accepted. Additional planning meetings were held in Berkeley and San Francisco in 1978 and early 1979 to address questions of funding, participant selection, and instructional methods. Concerning the last, it was agreed that the nature of the subject and the general maturity of the participants would require that a broad range of teaching devices be employed. Over MMI's first seven years these have come to include case studies (some real, some hypothetical), group exercises, role-playing, self-study instruments, films, videotapes, field trips, hands-on computer experience, the maintenance of daily journals, and extensive homework in addition to straight classroom lectures. Participants are also sent several written assignments to be completed before their arrival in Berkeley.

With additional support from the NEA, MMI undertook its first institute in July 1979. Since then, an annual institute has been held each summer, and—through the 1985 institute—the number of participants who have completed the program totals nearly 250. Ten of these have come from outside the United States: five from Canada, two from Australia, and one each from Israel, Mexico, and Venezuela. For all except the 1980 and 1981 institutes, the Chi Omega sorority house located on Piedmont Avenue and only a few minutes' walk from the Berkeley campus has been leased to serve as the program's residence.

While tuition charges cover a portion of the institute's annual operating expenses, from 1979 through 1983 the larger part of these had to be raised from a combination of outside sources. Joining with the NEA to help meet such expenses were the California Arts Council, the Hewlett, Donner, and Exxon foundations, and in 1982 and 1983, the J. Paul Getty Trust. As early as 1981, though, the AMAA had concluded that this piecemeal pattern of funding was not indefinitely sustainable and that the institute might have to be discontinued unless a more stable economic base could be established. Approaching the Getty Trust, the AMAA proposed that the latter take permanent responsibility for the program. Pending a decision, the trust provided partial interim funding for the two following summers while it commissioned a series of studies of MMI's curriculum, utility, effectiveness, and potential market. Satisfied by these that the program could make an important contribution to the vitality and stability of museums generally, the trust assumed MMI's full financial and operating responsibilities in 1984.

With but a few changes, the content of MMI's curriculum has remained remarkably close to the model first designed in 1977. Several topics (collective bargaining and space planning being two) have been dropped, a group of scattered sessions dealing with visitor surveys, public relations, membership, and development have been reorganized into a core concentration on marketing, and the classroom time devoted to working with computers has been doubled. In 1984 and 1985, the participants traveled to San Jose, California, to take a two-day executive computer training program given at the IBM Education Center.

The most important curriculum change, however, has involved sequencing rather than content. In the most recent institutes, the courses follow what might best be described as an ascending spiral in which the participants begin by concentrating on their personal roles in the management process (What assumptions do they bring to it? What are their preferred styles of learning? How do they best communicate?), then proceed to questions of management *inside* their institutions (How do they motivate others? How do they assure that resources are being used effectively and efficiently? How do budgets and other financial devices operate as systems of control?), and then, finally, move on to the management of their organizations in the *outside* world (What is strategic planning, and how can it best function in museums? What impact should local considerations have on program decisions? How do marketing concepts apply in a nonprofit setting? What are the uses and limits of public relations?). The culmination of this last phase is their immersion in a two-day-long integrative case study in which, working through their project teams, participants are asked to imagine themselves at some critical juncture in the evolution of a very real museum and to apply much of what they have learned during the three previous weeks.

While the MMI curriculum continues to be ostensibly free of museological concerns, an intimate familiarity with day-to-day museum operations nevertheless remains the warp across which most of its instruction is woven. In this connection, the participants' homogeneity of experience has proven an enormous advantage. Sharing many common assumptions, particularly about the centrality of collections and their care, they are able to work through museum-related case studies and other exercises with a confidence, skill, and depth of consideration that would not be possible for a more heterogeneous group which first needed to master the setting before it could address the underlying issues. That the participants have an immediate sense of what each other does has also proven an important element in creating an atmosphere of mutual respect. A registrar, for example, need say nothing more than that he or she is responsible for a collection of X million objects for the rest of an MMI class readily to understand just what such a job entails.

This homogeneity has also contributed significantly (and perhaps even more than the original planning committee has anticipated) to the intensity with which each summer's participants interact with one another and the dispatch with which they form themselves into a group convinced that its class is either the "best" or certainly the "most special" since the program's inception. This sense of cohesion and the energy it seems to engender have become important adjuncts to MMI's other instructional methods.

To strengthen this interaction further, and also to assure that loyalties continue to run toward the group overall rather than to any cliques within it, a number of adjustments have been made in recent years. For one thing, both breakfast and the evening meal are now served in the residence on a communal basis. Formerly, only breakfasts were eaten together, and who was to go out with whom for dinner—this frequently involved driving and tended to put the owners of cars in a momentarily advantageous social position—was sometimes an occasion for wounded feelings. Also, participants are assigned in advance to eight- or nine-person project teams which are changed each week so that every participant has the opportunity to work closely with as many other participants as possible. The requirement of residence, sometimes waived in the early days for those who lived in the Bay Area, is now strictly enforced. Finally, several evenings of information sharing have been introduced into the first week, enabling participants to project slides of exhibitions and other activities at their home institutions and to talk about their own career experiences and aspirations.

A fully evolved MMI class pursuing a case study late into the night and all but oblivious of any world beyond its Men's Faculty Club classroom and Chi Omega sorority house residence is an awesome sight. The energy released may also be one key to the program's success. To be sustained within MMI's protective ambit for a period of four weeks, surrounded wholly by colleagues absorbed in a common interest and generally free of the everyday duties of work and family life, becomes a unique opportunity for professional growth and learning. That this should come about nearly as much from the interchange among the participants as from their formal classroom instruction has become one of MMI's greatest strengths.

To advise the J. Paul Getty Trust not only with respect to MMI but also as to other future activities in the field of museum management training generally, the trust's president, Harold Williams, has recently appointed a Museum Management Advisory Committee composed of senior individuals from both within and outside the American museum community. With the additional experience, knowledge, and skill this group will bring to the planning process, the possibility now exists that some means might be devised to disseminate the instructional materials and methods developed for MMI to a larger audience and also—in response to a frequent demand from past MMI participants—that a series of "postgraduate" workshops might eventually be instituted. Making some broader use of MMI's materials and methods seems increasingly urgent as the demand for management training increases. MMI's 1985 institute attracted some 120 applications—a record number for any year— for the 35 places that were available. Many highly qualified applicants had to be turned away, and those accepted averaged more than eleven years of individual museum experience. That was also a record high.

The increases in the complexity of museums and their environment that initially impelled the need for management training have not abated. As it is currently constituted, MMI can meet only a fraction of the total demand. Its importance, however, ought not to be measured in numbers but rather by the efficacy of its innovations. MMI has become, and will continue to be, an important laboratory for the development of new ways through which dedicated museum professionals can be better equipped to take leadership positions within their own institutions and in the field. By helping to calm the apprehension so rampant in the time of its creation—the fear that museums had become too complicated to be managed by museum people—MMI can be said to have made an important contribution and provided an exemplary beginning.

AFTERWORD

In 1987 the AMAA merged into the American Federation of Arts, which continues to administer MMI. While some of the details of MMI itself have continued to change, its original purpose and shape have remained intact through to the plans for its 1990 offering.

REVIEW

The Arts and Public Policy in the United States

The Arts and Public Policy in the United States, edited by W. McNeil Lowry. Englewood Cliffs, New Jersey: Prentice-Hall, 1984, 196 pages, $7.95.

In the spring of 1984 the American Assembly convened a group of fifty-five individuals involved in the arts at Arden House in Harriman, New York, to examine "the factors that constitute public policy in the United States with respect to the arts, to locate the arts in our system of national values, and to assess the public and private actions that would make the status of the arts more secure in our society." This volume, *The Arts and Public Policy in the United States*, includes three background papers prepared for presentation at that assembly, the transcript of a preliminary symposium held the preceding December in New York City by a smaller group intended to be among the assembly's core participants, and introductory and concluding chapters by W. McNeil Lowry, retired vice president of the Ford Foundation's Division of Humanities and the Arts, who served both as moderator for the symposium and editor of the resulting publication. Also included is the brief

This book review first appeared in the *Journal of Arts Management and Law*, 15(2), Summer 1985, pp. 93–97.

"Final Report" issued at the assembly's conclusion.

Of these materials, the most provocative are the three background papers prepared by Stanley N. Katz, professor of public and international affairs at the Woodrow Wilson School of Princeton University; Perry T. Rathbone, senior vice president and director of Christie's International and director emeritus of the Museum of Fine Arts, Boston; and Paul J. DiMaggio, associate professor at Yale University's Institution for Social and Policy Studies. DiMaggio's paper, "The Nonprofit Instrument and the Influence of the Marketplace on Policies in the Arts," is particularly stimulating for its close analysis of how the substitution of one funding source for another may affect a recipient arts organization in ways that neither it nor its supporters intended or anticipated.

On the overarching issue of public policy, the participants appeared to agree that what most sharply distinguishes the situation of the arts in the United States from their situation in Europe is the lack of any single and centralized source of policy. We have neither established a ministry nor formulated a doctrine. What we have done instead is develop a *set* of policies that originate from a variety of sources, both public and private and both within the arts and beyond. (Not all of such policies have even been specifically intended to affect the arts; some examples cited by Katz include urban renewal, immigration, and tax policy.) That we have situated our cultural activity in the midst of "the push and pull of a multitude of conflicting public and private policies" should not, however, be taken as a sign of either abdication from or failure at the task of policy making. Rather, as Katz concludes:

[T]o have no policy is to have a policy. That we do not have a national cultural policy, in other words, means that we have made a decision (this going far back in our history) to leave to private and local institutions the determination of the decisions most overtly affecting the creation and conduct of cultural institutions.

While the participants were generally optimistic that this decentralization of policy making would continue to be a source of strength, they were not as sanguine about the current pattern of institutional support. A recurring concern was that dependence on the marketplace is having an increasingly detrimental effect on American arts organizations. Compared to Europe, the degree of market dependence in the United States is striking. According to an early 1970s study by Yale economist J. Michael Montias, earned income accounted for 54 percent of total arts organization revenues. The percentage was highest for large resident theaters, as much as 70 percent of their operating budgets. At the low end were art museums, local art and service organizations, and smaller minority arts organizations with figures ranging from 40 percent down. By contrast, the earnings of nonprofit performing arts organizations were 32 percent in France, 23 percent in Austria, 18 percent in Germany, and 11 percent in Sweden. As DiMaggio notes, the "extent to which American artists and artistic institutions are subject to the influence of the marketplace is virtually unparalleled in the developed world."

What is this influence, and how is it perceived as detrimental? The answer seems twofold. First, the marketplace is conservative. In the field of opera, for example, the degree to which experimental or contemporary works may be presented appears directly related to the degree that the performing company—most typically a conservatory or university group— is free from box office demands. Correspondingly, companies dependent on ticket sales for their survival will necessarily tend to produce the standard repertoire. As Peter Zeisler, director of the Theatre Communications Group and a participant in the symposium that preceded the Arden House Assembly, noted with some acerbity:

> We're in mid-December, and the artistic institutions in this country ground to a halt about three weeks ago because now the theatres are doing *A Christmas Carol,* the ballet companies are doing *Nutcracker Suite,* and in every museum the gift shops make

Bloomingdale's look like Korvette's. I can't believe this would happen at the Rijksmuseum.

In the Assembly's "Final Report," this position is stated more tersely: "An increasing tendency in art institutions and funding sources to rely upon earned income to bridge the gap between income and expenses risks compromising the artistic process."

Such reliance on the marketplace was secondarily perceived as detrimental to the extent that it tempts arts organizations toward specifically seeking out an affluent audience that can more readily afford a higher priced ticket or admission. Publicity costs the same, regardless of where it is aimed. Directing it upscale will consistently produce a better return than would aiming it down. DiMaggio sums it up thus:

> [A]t least two conclusions are worthy of confidence. First, the logic of the marketplace is in many ways inimical to the efforts of nonprofit arts organizations to present innovative productions and exhibitions of the sort favored by many artists, curators, and critics. Second, the marketplace is unsupportive of policies that expand the social range of the audience for the arts, serve the poor, or pursue the goal of public education.

With respect to funding, earned income was not the participants' only source of concern. Several also addressed the matter of *unearned* income and pointed out that a growing share of such income is coming in the form of institutional (that is, foundation, corporate, and government) support rather than individual patronage. With some poignance, Rathbone recalls that the Museum of Fine Arts in Boston was just short of its centenary when such a change in its funding pattern required that it remove from its rotunda "the longstanding magisterial inscription in gold letters: Museum of Fine Arts. / Founded, Built, and Maintained / Entirely with the Gifts of / Private Citizens."

Katz considers the consequence of this change in his background paper. When personal pleasure or a private passion is no longer the driving force behind patronage, then neither can a private judgment as to a project's potential artistic merit serve as an adequate basis for deciding whether to fund it. Tracing the growth of governmental subsidies for the arts, Katz concludes that "the price tag for this 'public' support is a swelling demand for public accountability." More often than not, such accountability has focused on process as much as on product.

Whereas a Henry Lee Higginson or J. P. Morgan was answerable to nobody but his inner muse—a muse that was perhaps more arbitrary than our nostalgia allows—this cannot be the case for a foundation (or corporate) giving officer or a government official. For the latter, a supplicant arts organization must necessarily be able to provide a solidly prepared application, an impeccable budget, and an unassailable final report. Says DiMaggio:

> The use of administrative and quantitative criteria for the evaluation of applications, a phenomenon extending to coporate donors, some private foundations, and government agencies, is less an expression of political will than a reflection of bureaucratic imperatives.

While that may be inevitable, and might in the long run even be good, it has nonetheless required corresponding changes (some subtle, some not so) in the way that arts organizations are managed. These may range from whom to hire ("Should we look for a grant writer instead of a second lighting designer?") to what program decisions are made ("Can we jazz up that new *Hamlet* with an outreach component?"). Commenting on this altered balance between artistic and managerial concerns, one of the symposium's participants observed ruefully, "[T]he tail is not wagging the dog now. The tail *is* the dog."

Another question raised—a surprising one for somebody like me who works in the museum field where institutionalization is not merely the traditional way of life but may actually be its raison d'etre—was whether the evolution of performing arts groups into the form of nonprofit organizations (an evolution necessary if they were to receive tax-deductible contributions) has not carried too great a price. Lowry remarks at one point that "this nonprofit beast is not yet understood" and at another point expresses doubt that in the case of the performing arts, the duration of such institutions should extend beyond the "life or career of one artistic director."

Underlying this concern is a deeper question about the power and influence of self-perpetuating, volunteer, community-based boards of trustees, the virtually inevitable concomitant of enterprises that cast themselves in the form of nonprofit organizations. Most outspoken here was Barbara Weisberger, the founder and former artistic director of the Pennsylvania Ballet. Expressing total confidence in the continuing vitality of artists—"I think they will persist . . . out of their own necessity and out of their own sense of purpose and commitment"—she was nonetheless concerned whether artists or even art itself could truly continue to flourish "within the institution."

This by no means exhausts the matters considered in *The Arts and Public Policy in the United States*. Beyond such questions as the locus of policy making, the impact of various forms of support, and the appropriateness of particular organizational forms, the participants also touched on such related issues as the training of artists, the better integration of the arts into public education, and the achievement within arts organizations of a more satisfactory balance between managerial competence and artistic aspiration. Whether the Arden House participants wholly succeeded in meeting their mandate is unclear. That their meeting had a valuable outcome is nonetheless certain. Without offering definite answers, this American Assembly publication will clearly strengthen our ability to deal with the important issues which were raised and, more often than not, freshly illuminated.

REPOSE AND OTHER
BRIEF LEGAL NOTES

REPOSE

The dictionary defines the word "repose" to mean a state of rest—the condition of being free from unsettling activity.

The legal sense in which it's used here is very similar. It will mean that condition in which you—as the putative owner and current possessor of a work of art or other object—need no longer fear that some successful claim of ownership might unexpectedly be asserted from out of some hitherto obscure past to deprive you of a valuable or irreplaceable object for which you may have paid a substantial purchase price and in which you may have invested substantial care. Put more tersely, "repose" will mean to be secure in possession of those objects of which you believe yourself to be the owner.

The law favors repose. By a variety of mechanisms it seeks to bar claims that are ancient or stale. As a matter of general policy, those who have claims are encouraged to come forward to assert them promptly. As a matter of fairness to those who must defend such claims, the law provides that they should have the chance to do so before—in the words of one commentator—"evidence has been lost, memories have faded, and witnesses have disappeared."

This article first appeared in *IFAR reports,* 8(6), August/September 1987.

For these reasons, our Anglo-American legal system includes statutes of limitation. A statute of limitation provides that
the right to begin a particular legal action is circumscribed by the
requirement that it be commenced within a particular time. If it is
not commenced in such a timely fashion, then we refer to the
action as barred. The law assigns a significant role to statutes of
limitations. As one court has explained:

> The statute of limitations is a statute of repose. At times it may bar
> the assertion of a just claim. Then its application causes hardship.
> The Legislature has found that such occasional hardship is out-
> weighed by the advantage of outlawing stale claims. (*Schmidt* v.
> *Merchants Dispatch Transp. Co.*, 270 N.Y. 287, 302, 200 N.E.
> 824, 827–828 (1936)).

Ordinarily, the statute of limitations pertinent to any claim will
begin to run at the time that the claim first accrues. Thus, if a
museum visitor slips on a wet gallery floor and breaks a leg, the
statute of limitations—generally something between two and six
years—would begin to run at the time of the injury. In the overwhelming number of instances, this has proven to be a satisfactory arrangement. Even if the full extent of the injury is not
initially known, the injured party will at least be aware (a) that he
has a cause of action, and (b) who it is that he can sue.

In at least two situations, however, this formulation does not
provide a satisfactory outcome. The first is where the potential
claimant is not immediately aware that any injury has occurred.
The classic case involves the surgeon who may have negligently
left a sponge or other object inside a patient. Should such a
patient be barred from suit because the statute of limitations may
have run before the injury ever comes to light? To rectify such a
potential injustice, the law has developed a so-called "discovery"
rule under which the statute of limitations may not begin to run
until the patient discovers the injury. In some states, a similar
"discovery" rule is applied in the case of fraud. Rather than
commencing to run at the time of a fraudulently induced transaction, the statute of limitations may not begin to run until the

aggrieved party has discovered the fraud—or, at least, should reasonably have discovered it.

The second instance in which the normal formulation—a statute of limitations that begins to run at the time of the injury—does not provide a satisfactory outcome is when the aggrieved party *does* know that he's been injured but does *not* know whom he can sue in order to rectify that injury. The stolen work of art is a classic case in point.

An object is stolen from your museum. Many years later it surfaces in the hands of a private collector or another museum who claims to have purchased it in good faith. Can you get it back? Or to reverse the situation, your museum purchases an object in good faith, conserves it and cares for it. Many years later, a private collector demands its return on the grounds that it had earlier been stolen from his collection. Must you give it back? In the normal course, under our Anglo-American legal system, the original owner would have the right to recover the stolen object regardless of the good faith in which it was later acquired. The law school rubric by which we describe this is: "You can't get good title from a thief."

In fact, however, if the statute of limitations applicable to an action to recover the stolen object has run, you may indeed be able to get what is the functional equivalent of a very good title either directly or indirectly from a thief. If the original owner is barred from recovering the object, then your ability to possess it may, for all practical purposes, be permanent. A key question in any such situation will be whether the statute of limitations pertinent to the original owner's right to recover the object began to run at the time of the theft or began to run at some later time. In California, for example, to cover situations such as this the legislature has recently adopted something almost exactly comparable to the "discovery" rule that was previously referred to with respect to certain kinds of negligence and fraud. In the case of an action to recover possession of a stolen art work, there is a three-year statute of limitations which does not begin to run until "the discovery of the whereabouts of the art."

That, however, is only one of the possible solutions to this problem. When a stolen object surfaces in the possession of a good faith purchaser, in all there are at least four different and distinct events that might be used to trigger the running of the applicable statute of limitations.

First: The statute might begin to run at the time of the theft. As suggested earlier, from the point of view of the original owner this clearly would be a harsh rule. The statute of limitations might easily have expired before the original owner is ever able to identify the party to be sued for the object's recovery.

Second: The statute might begin to run when the stolen object first comes into the hands of a good faith purchaser. This approach is employed in a number of "repose" proposals that have been advanced in recent years. It can also be found in Section 312 of the Convention on Cultural Property Implementation Act—better known as the UNESCO Implementation Act— that became federal law in 1983. Often coupled with this approach is the further refinement that the period of the statute of limitations will be shorter when the stolen object is held in such circumstances that its possession might easily become public knowledge. For the original owner, however, the defect remains that—as with the first alternative—the statute of limitations may already have expired before the original owner is able to identify the party in possession of the stolen object.

Third: The statute might begin to run when the original owner discovers—or reasonably could be expected to discover— the whereabouts of the stolen object. As noted earlier, this is today the law in California and was basically the approach taken some seven years ago by the New Jersey Supreme Court in the well-known Georgia O'Keeffe case (*O'Keeffe* v. *Snyder,* 416 A2d 862 (1980)) with the added requirement there that the owner must also have been diligent in seeking out the object.

Fourth: The statute might begin to run only after the original owner had discovered the whereabouts of the stolen object, demanded its return and then had this demand refused. This is currently the rule in New York (*Menzel* v. *List,* 298 NY2d 979 (1969)) and it is clearly the one most favorable to the original owner.

As should be evident, these alternatives form a continuum that begins with the rule most heavily weighted toward the good faith purchaser (a statute of limitations that begins to run at the time of the theft) and ends with the rule most heavily weighted toward the original owner (a statute that does not begin to run until there has been a demand and refusal).

Given this continuum, at what point along it might we— both as people protective of the interests of museums but also, presumably, as people sensitive to the interests of others— propose that the statute of limitations pertinent to the recovery of stolen art and other objects ought properly begin to run? In responding to that question, we must of course be mindful that in some instances our museums may be the aggrieved original owner from which these objects were stolen. In others, our museums may be the subsequent and good faith purchasers who have long held these objects in their collections. With that as a given, perhaps our best answer should be a "disinterested" one. The best statute of limitations would be one that struck the fairest balance possible between the parties.

Those within the museum community who have thus far worked most energetically for the adoption of "repose" legislation have taken the position that such a "disinterested" answer would be one that gave virtually equal weight to the rights of the original owner and those of the subsequent good faith purchaser. They argue that this is fair because the original owner is not the only victim in the stolen art situation. In fact, they say, there are actually two innocent and injured parties.

First, of course, there is the original owner whose property has been stolen. But second, there is the subsequent good faith purchaser who may have cared for the property for many years and may have invested substantial sums in its conservation and restoration. Not only does he stand to lose a valued and possibly irreplaceable object acquired in good faith but—if he is unable to recover from his vendor—he may stand to lose its purchase price as well.

That both parties are victims, I think we can agree. But are they equally innocent victims? I would argue that they are not. The position of the original owner is entirely an involuntary one. He has done nothing except to be robbed. The good faith purchaser, by contrast, has voluntarily entered into a transaction to acquire material of a type that is known sometimes to be problematic. Beyond this, he will have had the opportunity to request and receive documentation. He will have had the opportunity to negotiate an arrangement under which he might protect himself against the economic consequences of a subsequent third party claim. He will have had the opportunity to weigh the vendor's reputation. The purchasers with whom we are dealing here—and museum purchasers in particular—are not for the most part unsophisticated. If such a purchaser fails to acquire documentation or to secure his own economic interest or to confine himself to dealing with reputable vendors, then in an extreme case we might even question whether he really is a "good faith" purchaser at all. Even if we conclude that he is, it still remains clear that he has been willing to hazard a certain level of risk. It is unfair to expect that those who take such risks will at least sometimes have to suffer the attendant consequences?

If that analysis is correct, then our "disinterested" answer to the question of when a statute of limitations should begin to run might be one that is still protective of both parties but inclines somewhat more toward the original owner than toward the subsequent purchaser. They are both victims, but the former would appear to be more the innocent victim than does the latter.

AFTERWORD

Until 1987, there was perhaps no statute of limitations as favorable to the original owner and as adverse to the subsequent good faith purchaser as that of New York. There, the statute of limitations did not begin to run until the original owner had learned the whereabouts of the stolen property, demanded its return, and then had that demand refused. This rule was dramatically (and controversially) turned around in *DeWeerth* v. *Baldinger,* a case decided in December 1987 by the federal Second Circuit Court of Appeals. The new New York rule focuses on something entirely different—not demand and refusal but the diligence with which the original owner attempts to locate and procure the return of the stolen property.

As thus interpreted, this new rule may be just as adverse to the original owner as the old rule was to the subsequent good faith purchaser. Its impact can clearly be seen in a 1989 decision involving the Guggenheim Museum. In the mid-1960s, the museum noted that a small painting by Marc Chagall could not be located in storage. A formal inventory of the collection taken in 1969 confirmed that this painting was, indeed, missing.

Meanwhile, however, and unbeknownst to the museum, the painting had surfaced on the New York City art market. In 1967, it was purchased by a couple named Lubell from the highly reputable Madison Avenue dealer Robert Elkon. In 1986, the Guggenheim learned for the first time of the painting's whereabouts and demanded its return. Mrs. Lubell (Mr. Lubell having died in the interim) refused, and a lawsuit followed.

In its 1989 decision, the New York Supreme Court ruled that Mrs. Lubell could keep her painting. Applying the new rule that emerged from the *DeWeerth* decision, the court reasoned as follows:

> Whether a party has acted with due diligence may be a question of law for the court to decide. . . . In this case, the facts are undisputed: plaintiff did nothing for twenty years except search its premises, although its director knew of the agencies which are routinely contacted when a work of art is missing (e.g. N.Y.C. Police Department, Federal Bureau of Investigation, Interpol and the Art Dealers' Association).
>
> The diligence required increases with the value of the lost property. If, as in the present case, the property is art work by a

famous painter, with substantial value, a major search effort may reasonably be expected. . . . The Guggenheim's efforts were minimal, much less than that of the plaintiff in the *DeWeerth* case, [and] inadequate in view of the value of the painting. For that reason, the motion [to dismiss] is granted on the ground that the statute of limitations bars the action.

That the *Guggenheim* case might have been decided otherwise as recently as two years earlier seems likely. As it *was* decided, however, it certainly sounds a sharp warning that—whatever the past practice may have been—a museum in New York, and perhaps elsewhere, that fails to report a loss to the authorities and to make every other reasonable effort to recover its missing property is running a considerable risk. If that property should subsequently surface in the hands of a good faith purchaser, then the museum may have lost it forever.

WHO OWNS THE NATARAJA?

During the past decade, demands for the repatriation of works of art—or of objects that we in the West consider art—have increased from a murmur to a clamor. Greece, Thailand, Turkey, Nigeria, Peru, and Romania are just a few of the countries that have recently sought the return of artifacts held by Western museums and other collectors for years, decades, or even centuries. Such claims raise a host of thorny legal, ethical, and public policy issues—ones that might better be resolved within the framework of international consensus rather than on a case-by-case basis.

Nothing could better illustrate the vagaries of such a piecemeal approach than a case decided in February of last year in Britain's High Court of Justice. At issue was a twelfth-century Shiva Nataraja—a bronze Hindu icon depicting Shiva as Lord of the Dance—purchased by a Canadian collector from a London art dealer in 1982 for roughly $405,000.

The Indian government commenced a proceeding for the Nataraja's recovery. India's claim was twofold. First, it said, the Nataraja was the same figure that a "landless labourer" named Ramamoorthi had unearthed and unlawfully removed in 1976

ARTnews, 88(5), May 1989. This was originally written as a column for the magazine's "Perspective" series.

from the site of a long-ruined temple near the village of Pathur in the state of Tamil Nadu. Second, said India, there must be some party with a title to the icon superior to that of its good faith Canadian purchaser. Perhaps this rightful owner was India or Tamil Nadu; perhaps it was the long-ruined temple or, alternately, a public official appointed to look after the temple's affairs; most astonishingly, perhaps it was the god Shiva himself, as he was "localized" in the Shiva Lingam, a stone symbolizing Shiva's generative powers that was once the focus of the temple's worship.

The trial lasted more than forty days. As for India's first claim, the presiding Justice Kennedy found that the Nataraja purchased in 1982 *was* the same bronze that Ramamoorthi—brought in as a witness—had unearthed. But to whom did this icon now belong? For it was once part of a suite of Shiva figures that had been buried centuries earlier.

To reach a decision, Kennedy embarked on a fascinating journey through Hindu law, theology, and custom. His point of departure was the establishment of the temple in the twelfth century and the fact that it had borne a donor's name. Assuming this donor's intent was pious, then the temple's central focus—the Shiva Lingam—could be treated as the continuing and still-present embodiment of that intent. Under Hindu law, the lingam could also be considered a juristic entity, capable of holding property, of suing, and of being sued. It no more strained credulity, the judge said, that an idol could own property in India than that a corporation—also a legal fiction—could do so in England. Thus, the god Shiva himself, as manifest in the lingam, could be treated as the rightful owner of the Nataraja. Alternately, the temple, although abandoned, might itself be deemed the ongoing personification of the donor's pious intent and as such also considered the juristic entity that still "owned" the Nataraja.

The defendant's advocates fired off their own theological artillery. If the Nataraja embodied certain aspects of Shiva's divinity, they asked, how could it be property in the sense that one of the Indian parties could claim title to it in an English court or even refer to it as stolen? Did not the fact of its consecration put it above the reach of the court and beyond such mundane questions as ownership and possession?

However, Kennedy opted instead for the more expansive view urged by India. The Nataraja, he said, could at once possess divine qualities and still, while not being "mere property in the crude sense," remain a piece of bronze. In the end, he awarded the Nataraja to the temple. The Canadian collector, who received no compensation, has planned to appeal. Whatever reparations he might have been owed by the London dealer would in no way compensate for the cost of the trial.

As legal decisions go, the High Court's is exotic, even poetic. For museums and other collectors, though, it is also unsettling. Their collections hold the products of a variety of cultures, each with its own cosmology, customs, and law. In determining how public funds can be spent and what may be properly acquired and displayed, could any museum curator or collector master the multitude of legal nuances that lurk beneath this diversity? Far better would be a strengthened, more predictable, and more encompassing international mechanism to deal with such claims.

A good starting point might be the 1970 UNESCO Convention on the "Means of Prohibiting and Preventing the Illicit Import, Export and Transfer of Ownership of Cultural Property." While permitting a broad range of recoveries, Article 7 of the convention also recognizes the principle that in certain cases—the Nataraja case might well have been one—"just compensation" ought be paid to what the convention terms "an innocent purchaser." In our sample case, the outcome might have differed if India had waited until the Nataraja had reached Canada: both countries ratified the UNESCO Convention. But India chose to sue in Great Britain, which had never become party to the convention.

Efforts to stop the outward flow of a nation's cultural heritage may be widely applauded. Attempts to reverse that flow by compelled repatriation should elicit a cooler response. That transactions in the international art market may have sometimes transformed one culture's heritage into another's commodity is both undeniable and regrettable. It does not, however, necessarily follow that redress can be had simply by undoing what has already been done. In preserving the objects of other cultures, and by making these objects publicly accessible, we have created a new situation. Our great Western collections have themselves become cultural artifacts.

Arching above once-individual cultures, there is today a collective cultural patrimony that has been formed by the flow, mingle, and merge of history. The potential dismantling of that patrimony is too profound a matter to be addressed in a haphazard way. Before more claims such as India's for the Nataraja begin to reach our own courts, we of the American collecting community would be well advised to consider how such international mechanisms as the UNESCO Convention (to which the United States is also a party) might be strengthened, extended, and made more exclusively applicable. What's at stake has become *our* heritage, too.

LEGAL ASPECTS OF THE
DISPLAY OF IMITATIONS

A s used herein, "imitation" means a superficially exact copy of an original work of
art fabricated by somebody other than the artist (or the artist's
designee) in the same scale and material as the original. Among
the rights that must be considered prior to the fabrication and
display of such an imitation in the United States are those of (a)
the owner of the original, (b) the copyright holder, (c) the artist,
(d) if the original depicts a human subject, any person so depicted, (e) the visitors to any exhibition in which the imitation is
to be displayed, and (f) the public generally. In addition, consideration must be given to whether such a display would affect the
exhibitor's classification as a "museum."

(a) *The rights of the owner of the original.* If the owner is
neither the copyright holder nor the artist—the situation that
prevails for most works of art created and sold in Europe at any
time or in the United States on or after January 1, 1978 (when the
new federal copyright law took effect)—then the owner's only

This paper was originally prepared for submission to the symposium *Originals and Substitutes in Museums,* convened by the International Committee
for Museology (ICOFOM) of the International Council of Museums,
Zagreb, Yugoslavia, October 1985. It first appeared in *ICOFOM Study
Series 8.*

means to prevent the fabrication of an unauthorized imitation would be by his control over access to the original. It has been argued that such control renders nugatory the right of the copyright holder to make or authorize reproductions and that a balance ought be struck between these rights. Concerning the public display of the imitation, the owner of the original would not, per se, have any right to prevent it.

(b) *The rights of the copyright holder.* If the original is still under copyright and the copyright holder is a person other than the artist—the situation that prevails for most works of art created and sold in the United States prior to January 1, 1978—then the copyright holder may at a minimum (1) enjoin the display of an unauthorized imitation as an infringement, and (2) claim damages for its fabrication. Also available may be such further sanctions as the seizure, judicial forfeiture, and destruction of such an imitation and of any implements, devices, or equipment used in its fabrication. Whether the exhibitor might successfully assert "fair use" as a defense would depend on such facts as who fabricated the imitation, the purposes for which it was to be used, and the continuing commercial availability or nonavailability of the original.

(c) *The rights of the artist.* If the artist (or, in the case of a recently deceased artist, the artist's heir or representative) holds the copyright, then, just as in the instance above, he may (1) enjoin the display of an unauthorized imitation, and (2) claim damages for its fabrication. Moreover, whether or not the artist holds the copyright, he may be able to prevent the display of an unauthorized imitation in New York or in any other state enacting a moral right law similar to New York's recent Artists' Authorship Rights Act. This proscribes the public display of a work of art or any *reproduction* thereof in an altered or modified form. The artist's assertion that the most minor inaccuracies of an unauthorized imitation constituted a modification of the original and that such modification was damaging to his reputation might well be sufficient to establish a cause of action. (While California and Massachusetts also have adopted moral right statutes in recent years, the artist would have no such remedy under these since only the physical alteration of an original work of art is actionable in those states.) As another remedy in New York and elsewhere, the artist might be able to require that his name be disassociated from such an imitation even if he cannot prevent its display. Finally, there is a possibility that the artist may claim that the display of an unauthorized imitation is an effort to "pass off" somebody else's work as his, i.e., that it constitutes a deceptive practice. *Gilliam* v. *American Broadcasting Companies, Inc.*, 538 F.2d 14 (2d Cir. 1976), which dealt with the unauthorized editing of a television program created by the Monty Python comedy group, involved such an analysis. The further telecasting of the program was enjoined under Section 43(a) of the federal Lanham Act on the grounds that it misrepresented the product of those who originally created it. Whether the Lanham Act could be applied in this way to the unauthorized display of an imitation work of visual art remains undetermined.

(d) *If the original work depicts a human subject, the rights of the person so depicted.* Unless the person portrayed has consented thereto, he may have recourse to prevent the display of an imitation through the right of privacy or the right of publicity. Under the latter, the heirs of such a person might also have a similar remedy given a recent trend to treat the right of publicity as surviving an individual's death and descendible. While a 1984 California statute extending this right for fifty years after death includes a specific exception for an *original* work of fine art, this exception would not apply to an imitation. Thus, an original oil painting of the late actress Marilyn Monroe might be exhibited by a museum in California but the display of an imitation would support an action for damages by Ms. Monroe's heirs. In the case of a work that is defamatory of the person portrayed, however, no such distinction need be drawn. The display of the imitation should not result in any different result than would the display of the original.

(e) *The rights of visitors to any exhibition in which such an imitation is to be displayed.* If the exhibitor of such an imitation, whether through misleading allegations or concealment, induces persons to visit such an exhibition in the belief that they are to view the original and they thereby suffer some detriment, then the exhibitor may be held liable in a civil action for fraud. Consider the instance of a group of tourists induced to travel on the representation that they are to see the original *Mona Lisa* when the object they are shown is, in fact, merely an imitation.

(f) *The rights of the public generally.* Beyond serving as the basis of a civil action for fraud, the fabrication and display of an imitation for deceptive purposes may also be treated as an offense to the public generally and prosecuted under the criminal laws of fraud, forgery, simulation, or counterfeiting. A subtler problem is raised by the imitation that is fabricated in good faith but could potentially find its way into the art market where it might be passed off as original. In *New York* v. *Wright Hepburn Webster Gallery, Ltd.,* 314 N.Y.S.2d 661 (Sup. Ct. N.Y.Co. 1970) the attorney general of New York asked the court to prevent (as a public nuisance) the sale of paintings created by one David Stein "in the style of" Braque, Klee, Miro, Chagall, Matisse, and Picasso on the grounds that Stein's name could easily be removed and the paintings thereafter sold as originals by those masters. The court refused to do so on the grounds that this had not yet occurred. Also, the fact that some individuals might subsequently be injured did not raise the defendant's conduct to the level of a public nuisance. Attacking this same problem and citing the damages done by the circulation of imitation art, professors Albert E. Elsen and John Henry Merryman of Stanford University proposed in 1979 that all countries adopt laws to control the fabrication of such imitations. In the case of paintings, drawings, fine prints, and other two-dimensional works, they would require that all reproductions be at least 25 percent larger or smaller than the original. In the case of sculpture, they would require either a change in the medium or a substantial change in scale. While such a solution might ease the danger of potential fraud, in some jurisdictions it would raise a moral right problem to the extent that a reproduction of a work of art might thereby be displayed in "altered" form. Finally, if the exhibitor was under some publicly imposed disability from displaying the original (if it was pornographic, for example, or displayed some federally protected image such as the Red Cross), he would be at least equally disabled from displaying the imitation.

The classification of the exhibitor as a "museum." Assuming all of the preceding difficulties can be overcome—i.e., that an institution is able to fabricate and display imitations with the full authority of every interested party, without deceiving the public, with adequate safeguards that such objects will not enter the stream of commerce, and without otherwise disturbing the public order—how would this affect the exhibitor's classification? To take the most extreme case, could an institution be classified as an art museum if its collection consisted wholly of imitations of original works of art currently extant in art museums elsewhere? Under the ICOM definition of 1974, to be classified as a museum an institution must acquire and display "material evidence of man and his environment." It is unlikely that a collection of imitations would be accorded the same evidentiary value as a collection of original works of art. If the accreditation rules of the American Association of Museums were applicable, classification as a museum is also questionable. Essential is the ownership and utilization of "tangible objects." These, in turn, are defined as having an "intrinsic value to science, history, art or culture . . . [that] must reflect . . . the museum's stated purpose." It may be deemed that imitations of extant works of art have no "intrinsic value" in an art museum (although the case might be wholly different in a museum dealing, for example, with the technology of reproduction). Such an imitation-filled institution might well be disqualified from obtaining certain tax benefits or from participating in various grant programs intended to benefit museums. At the other extreme, the presence in a museum's collection of a relatively small number of imitations would most likely be considered inconsequential.

In summary, under the laws of the United States the fabrication and display of imitations of works of art (and particularly of works of relatively recent origin) pose a number of legal considerations which ought be anticipated before an institution embarks on such a program. An institution that is given over wholly or substantially to the collection and display of imitations may be engaged in a legitimate educational activity (or even, as in the case of Disneyland, in providing a relatively harmless form of entertainment). In all likelihood, though, it cannot be classified as an art museum.

A MEDITATION ON WORK

The following is taken from remarks introducing Professor Howard Lesnick, Distinguished Professor of Law at the City University of New York Law School at Queens College. I have included it here because I believe Professor Lesnick's principal subject of inquiry—the possibility of restructuring the legal rules relevant to the workplace in order to reflect a greater range of potential relationships—has important connections to the concept of "professionalism" as it is developing in the museum field.

In an article entitled "When Work Isn't Work," published in *Parade* magazine (February 10, 1985), John Kenneth Galbraith called attention to the public policy consequences that ensue when we use the single word "work" to describe both what it is that people such as artists, scholars, business executives, scientists, and politicians do and the "hard, tedious, physically or mentally debilitating thing" that "men or women do in a factory, when picking fruits and vegetables on a farm, cleaning streets, staffing a sweatshop.

They so labor because they are paid; they would not dream of doing it otherwise."

From our middle-twenties to middle-sixties, working is what most of us spend more time doing than almost anything else. Whether of that sweated kind that Professor Galbraith says we would only do in exchange for wages or of that exalted kind which we tend to call a vocation or profession, it is work—truly—that saturates our lives.

And yet, when we come to talk about that work—and, more significantly, when as legislators, judges, directors, or managers we are called upon to make rules about it—the articulated assumptions from which we proceed have been remarkably narrow. Nowhere do they seem to take into account those extremely diverse way *in* which—and the multiple motives *from* which—human beings combine their efforts in a variety of enterprises that do more than simply increase the world's store of goods, in enterprises that may also give a richer meaning to the lives of those who are thus engaged. As Professor Lesnick wrote in 1983, "The prevailing consciousness of work sees work as an exchange relation, the giving up of leisure, the expending of effort, in return for compensation."

To add an observation of my own: if we turn to the West *Digest* to point us toward the decided cases that deal with the two central relationships of the workplace—those of employees with their employers and those of employees with one another—where must we look? Basically, we must go to the heading of "Master and Servant." It is a large one. In the *Ninth Decennial Digest,* the skeleton key listing alone covers more than a dozen pages.

Depending upon how literally we choose to take those words, we may be operating from assumptions even more narrow than those Professor Lesnick suggests. Central to the prevailing consciousness of work might be the notion that we not only surrender our leisure in return for compensation—either income or status or both—but that we also surrender our autonomy. The question here is not whether a degree of discipline is necessary for the effective functioning of an enterprise. Nobody would argue otherwise. The question, rather, is what happens when we locate the notion of obedience—the servant's chief duty to his or her master—at the very core of such workplace relationships. What happens, in short, when we choose as a model for this overwhelming occupation of our life something midway between a Prussion military organization and a well-run Medici palace?

Need we be so confined? Might there not be alternative and more expansive ways to envision the relationships that are formed around the nucleus of work? We are not dealing, after all, with some immutable aspect of nature. Work is a human arrangement that we as human beings can analyze, discuss, argue over, or agree about and—if we so will it—remodel to better suit our purposes. The need is for a construct that would initially let us think about work—and ultimately enable us to make rules about work—in ways that might be far richer and more satisfying than those available to us today.

Wittgenstein said that the limits of our language are the limits of our world. If we are to stretch the horizons of our working world, then we must begin by finding new words by which to describe it. We must overcome that current shortage of paradigms that can leave us thinking about our most committed effort as no more than a commodity we make available for sale, of our employers as our masters, and of those who work with and assist us as our servants. We need to explore other models.

ART, LAW, AND UTOPIA

In 1945, in a talk he gave over the BBC to celebrate the formation of the Arts Council of Great Britain, John Maynard Keynes—the council's first chairman—spoke of the work of the artist. It is, by its nature, he said,

> individual and free, undisciplined, unregimented, uncontrolled. The artist walks where the breath of the spirit blows him. He cannot be told his direction; he does not know it himself. But he leads the rest of us into fresh pastures and teaches us to love and enjoy what we often begin by rejecting, enlarging our sensibility and purifying our instincts. . . .

For those of us who have had the privilege to work closely with art and with artists, I think this will sound right. From every artist, we expect a certain mastery, a trained and professional skill in dealing with his or her material. But from the artist of larger gifts, we expect something more. We expect that he or she will use this professional skill not merely to amuse, to entertain,

---

These remarks were prepared for a conference of the Washington Area Lawyers for the Arts held at the Hirshhorn Museum and Sculpture Garden in December 1983, when the museum was exhibiting *Dreams and Nightmares: Utopian Visions in Modern Art.*

or even to move us but, beyond that, to make us—in George Bernard Shaw's grand phrase—"dream of things that never were"—to lead us toward new ways in which to imagine our lives and to understand the lives of those around us. Such an artist, truly, has the power to enlarge our sensibilities, to purify our instincts, and to help each of us lead a more richly varied and satisfying life.

But what of the converse? Is there any reciprocal gift, something beyond our own professional mastery of legal practice, beyond our own basic technical skills as draftsmen, negotiators, or litigators, that we in turn might bring to the artists with whom we work? Is there some corresponding enlargement of *their* sensibility to which *we*—as attorneys—might contribute? I think that there is, and—by one of those strange but wonderful coincidences—I think that the exhibition you will find installed in the gallery adjoining this auditorium suggests just what that contribution might be.

Entitled *Dreams and Nightmares: Utopian Visions in Modern Art* and organized by Valerie Fletcher of the Hirshhorn Museum staff, this exhibition attempts to trace some of the ways in which twentieth-century artists were at first enchanted—and then later repelled—by the vision of a harmonious society from which every trace of roughness, contingency and conflict had forever been banished.

As lawyers, of course, we know a good bit about roughness, contingency, and conflict. They lie, in fact, at the heart of our trade. And among the things we know about them, there are some that seem to me of transcendant importance:

We know, for example, that every conflict is not, as the utopian visionaries once projected, the sign of some systemic dysfunction. On the contrary, we know that in a free society such conflicts may be nothing more than the inevitable consequence of the legitimately differing interests which constitute the very fabric of such a society.

We know, too, that there will often be conflicts that can only be dealt with by temporizing measures that still leave their final disposition unresolved but permit the world to get on with its business. In contrast to the utopian urge toward the pure, definite, finality of a Mondrian grid, we have learned to make constructive use of what others may sometimes perceive as blurred, shaded, or even fuzzy.

And we know, finally, that given the choice between an ongoing process of conflict resolution and a situation in which every clash of interests has finally and permanently been resolved, the latter can only be embraced at great peril. The utopian vision, no matter how alluring, is ultimately the vision of a society in which roughness, contingency, and conflict have been and must repeatedly again be repressed—and such a society is not by our standards a decent society.

Here, then—to supplement the technical skills that we can offer—might be that special and reciprocal contribution which we, as attorneys, could make to the artists with whom we work: our understanding that differences of opinion may truly be genuine and not simply the product of malice or ignorance, that provisional solutions—no matter how unacceptable they may be in the making of art—may truly be useful in the living of life, and finally, and perhaps most importantly, that there will be times when the way a thing is done will be more important that what is done.

It will not, I hope, be thought presumptuous to suggest that these are important things to know and that, so far as we can help our artist friends to learn them better, then we in turn will have made a very real contribution to *their* understanding of that everyday world in which they must do their work and secure their livelihood. It seems like a fair exchange.